About the Author

Kathryn is the third daughter of David and Laura; the subjects of this book. Their children, are what has been termed ABC's or "American Born Chinese." As you read their parents' story, you will discover a world of implied and overtly demonstrated racism, often whispered, silently levied with a glance or stare, and, as is the case in this story, cruelly applied in unthinkable ways.

GWAIPO – A Forbidden Love Story

Kathryn P. Fong

GWAIPO – A Forbidden Love Story

Olympia Publishers
London

www.olympiapublishers.com
OLYMPIA PAPERBACK EDITION

Copyright © Kathryn P. Fong 2023

The right of Kathryn P. Fong to be identified as author of this work has been asserted in accordance with sections 77 and 78 of the Copyright, Designs and Patents Act 1988.

All Rights Reserved

No reproduction, copy or transmission of this publication may be made without written permission.
No paragraph of this publication may be reproduced, copied or transmitted save with the written permission of the publisher, or in accordance with the provisions of the Copyright Act 1956 (as amended).

Any person who commits any unauthorized act in relation to this publication may be liable to criminal prosecution and civil claims for damage.

A CIP catalogue record for this title is available from the British Library.

ISBN: 978-1-80074-993-1

This is a work of fiction.
Names, characters, places and incidents originate from the writer's imagination. Any resemblance to actual persons, living or dead, is purely coincidental.

First Published in 2023

Olympia Publishers
Tallis House
2 Tallis Street
London
EC4Y 0AB

Printed in Great Britain

Dedication

This book is dedicated to my father and mother, David and Laura.

Acknowledgements

Nothing comes from a vacuum of thought, and no one can attempt to write something worthwhile without the help of others, whether in the form of actively reading or editing, or just providing encouraging words to help you find a way around obstacles. Words of encouragement have meant so much to me over the course of writing this book. To my dear friend, Marilyn Baird: you never disappoint. You are always, always there for me, saying the right words, lifting my spirit up, reinforcing my faltering steps. You were my very first beta reader and my last editor. You made me discover how much I love to use the comma! With your kind and supportive words, you led me to my 1,000th revision and a whole new perspective. You made this possible, and I Love you. To my dear friends, Liz Brewer Casperson and Melanie Brewer Nielson: You were bright enough to ask what I was doing, and when I shared with you my stories, you grabbed on to me and would not let go. Both of you have provided me the "cheering section," I needed to focus and finish. I love you both, and never let me go! To S. Gary-Gary whose background in Old and New Cantonese and Chinese customs in general, helped me to establish time and context, as well as Chinese names I needed to know because I am too "ABC" and therefore, handicapped in my knowledge of my own Chinese heritage. (ABC means "American-Born Chinese.") To my Nephew Christopher Scott Bell: You picked up a fallen Old Lady and finished the race for her. I cannot thank you enough for caring about this book to give it all your eager attention. We will share this success together for Grandma and Grandpa Fong. Thank you for all you have done to support, encourage and direct my path toward success. And finally, to my BFF and Sister, Vickie Rae Eldredge: For over a quarter of a century you never left my side, you never let go of our friendship and you never stopped loving me. You held me when I shed tears, you laughed with me through good times, and you picked me up every time I faltered, fell or needed help to move on. You have done so much for me, and I could not have asked for a better friend, sister or mentor. You're the family I needed.

Gwaipo (pronounced as *Gwai Po*) is a Chinese Cantonese slang term for a White Western woman. It refers to a White female as a "White Ghost" or "White Devil" and has a history of racially deprecatory use.

GWAILO refers to White Western Males, or collectively, all White persons in general.

With a world war waging in the background, two people, one a beautiful blue-eyed Caucasian, the other a handsome, charismatic Chinese, met and fell in love, bringing a cascade of unforgiving cruelty down on their heads.

This work has been, for the most part, fictionalized; however, the events are based on real life events, people and places that affected the lives of our mother and father.

Treatment

My mother was a Caucasian woman who met and married my father, a man born in China. In their 1940's era, the right to love did not exist.

My father was sold as a baby and brought into this country as an indentured servant at age six. He was raised by an evil man who hated White people and who treated my father as his slave until the day this evil man died.

My mother had braced herself for the prejudice and judgments expected by her family and friends, and even strangers, but she was not prepared for what her Chinese in-laws would say, or more cruelly, do to her. She was "Gwaipo" meaning "White Devil" to them.

They married, and because they married, they were in for the fight of their lives.

Here then, is their "forbidden" love story for all the world to see.

Introduction

I have a story to tell. It is a story of hate and betrayal, of love and loss. And yes, it speaks to our Racial History, but even more so, it reveals itself to be a forbidden love story and yet, a true story of enduring courage. It is the story of my mother and my father: two disparate people who met at the very height of World War II. With this world war waging in the background, two people, one a beautiful blue-eyed Caucasian, the other a handsome, charismatic Chinese, met and fell in love, bringing a cascade of unforgiving cruelty down on their heads.

How can I possibly make you understand? You have little to no idea what it was like back then. Your generation has only heard stories. You've taken things for granted in your world. Everybody, it seems nowadays, "hooks up" or marries any one they please, without consequence, without the scorn of older generations, without the smirks and derisions of friends and family. Some families and friends dare not "speak" their innermost thoughts and feelings. It has been said that until you understand how it "feels" to be a victim of racial prejudice, you know nothing about it. Empathy notwithstanding, you must understand how it must feel like; otherwise, you cannot fathom the depths of such judgment, ugliness, and pain.

How can I make you understand what I barely understood myself?

When you grieve the loss of a loved one, it generally strikes you that you don't fully understand the person who just died at all, leaving you always to ask "why?" It's a dissatisfying question: "why?" In most cases, you never get an answer, so the "why" lingers, fades for a while, then re-emerges to nudge you or prick you into asking once again, "why?"

It is the one lingering question I have after the death of my parents. "Why?" Not "why did they die?" But "Why did they fall in love in the first place?" Who does that in 1944, when one of the biggest world wars was raging at its peak; when hundreds of thousands of Asians were being interred in camps all over the west, and when Chinese Americans could not leave the confines of their Chinatown district enforced by a military curfew? They couldn't even get a license to marry in the State of California, whose laws, at the time, did not permit interracial marriage.

Because I never understood why my parents married, I never understood, nor could I even imagine, their love for one another. Their relationship confused me all my life. I did not know, nor had I ever felt their love for one another. Who were they to fall in love and marry? Who was I to judge their love, or even try to measure it? Because I had no clear vision of who they were as lovers, I could not validate and defend their marriage against all reason.

My own confusion started at a very young age: I was about five or six years old, sitting in our 1938 black Buick with my two older sisters, parked at a curb in Oakland's Chinatown. My sisters and I were waiting for our father to come out of the grocery store where he bought his Chinese groceries. I was ignoring the play and chatter of my two older sisters, as I stood looking at all the passersby, most of whom were Asian. A strange thought occurred to my young and innocent mind as I watched the faces of those passing our car. "How can they see out of their squinty eyes," I thought. My fingers went to the corners of my eyes and pulled back my lids so that I could barely make out anything. My young mind could not figure out how Asians could see out of their narrow and heavy-lidded eyes. When my sisters turned to see what I was doing, it quickly became a game as we pulled our eyes back with our fingers and made faces at the Asians passing by. We didn't comprehend what we were doing.

On another occasion, when, once again, my sisters and I were left in the car, parked at the curb near Chinatown, we were startled by a young, bearded man, a Caucasian, with brown hair and blue eyes, dressed in a dirty trench coat. He was yelling at us, pointing at us from across the street, though we did not clearly hear what he was saying as he pointed to us. He finally made a rush for our car, crossing the street, all the while yelling at us, and stopping long enough to reach down into the gutter, scooping up dirt, mud and leaves and hurled the debris at our car. A moment later, he moved on, having done what he intended and he continued walking away from us down the sidewalk toward Oakland's Chinatown.

Though I was too young to understand, and too young to realize that I (and my sisters) were just targeted by a bigot, it was my first encounter with a white person who had little tolerance for Asians. I was even too young to realize I was part Asian. It never occurred to me that I was the same as those Chinese people who passed our car. I did not know that some people did not like Asian people, nor did I comprehend why.

It was the same confusion I had about the love my parents had for each other.

For me, love was rarely displayed before my youthful eyes. I did not see it. My ears did not hear it. Words were not used to express it in our home. I did not see it in birthday presents, or Christmas gifts, and nothing came to me in the guise of love, for the purpose of love, or as confirmation of love for me.

I have no occipital lobe, meaning that my skull lacks a beautiful curve most human beings enjoy at the back of their heads. The back of my skull is totally flat. This is indicative of an infant laying in their crib far too long. It reflects the fact that I, as an infant, was not picked up and held enough to prevent my skull bones from flattening as they knitted together. I apparently proved of little annoyance; Mother used to tell me how I would "coo" for hours in a self-soothing tone, amusing myself, entertaining myself, and crying only when absolutely necessary. Even my cries, she told me, were soft like a mewling kitten. My self-soothing habits served me well then as a baby and have proven a worthy gift as an adult living alone.

Mother's frame of mind before and after my birth was foretelling of all the pain she felt after our father, and her husband, returned from China. Thereafter, her pain would never leave her.

I was young yet, perhaps too young, when I first realized my mother did not want me. She didn't want any children. The trail of her woe on the subject was made manifest in photographs she did not take of me. How odd that I should find confirmation in the lack of photos, but there it is: My two older sisters had a chronology of baby pictures heralding their births. The photographs, black and white, small and on paper that had white ruffled borders, showed a loving parent holding a small bundle of baby, wrapped warm in receiving blankets, its eyes squinting tightly against light and sun. By the time I came along, the third child born of reconciliation, remorse, regret, and pain, I failed to produce in them any pride or heraldry; certainly not enough to warrant taking a photograph of me. There are no pictures announcing my birth, and you would not know I existed as a *family member in photos until about the age of three. Yes, copious baby pictures of my three younger brothers whose births followed mine revived my mother, but parents take pride in baby boys, don't they? I was born the year after my 'father's infamous return from China. It was a trip that tore at them both, from the inside, leaving scars that would last a lifetime. It was at this time Mother's life changed. The fire of defiance that saw her through her initial romance with Daddy had cooled. Her imagination reeled over and over with the realization that her husband returned not just an adulterer, but also a bigamist. The thought of what her Chinese In-laws were capable of doing to eliminate her and their marriage rocked her with waves and waves of crushing reality. Mother would never recover either her life before he left for China, nor the permanent pain she felt throughout the remainder of her life.*

I was born from that pain. Yet, I was part of a family, and as a daughter, and a sister, I held a place that was cocooned in a nest lightly feathered in love, I suppose. I, no matter how awkwardly expressed, nor how lacking in substance it came to me, knew that I was somehow loved. It came as a sense of belonging, a sense of Family, and, at times, a sense of wholeness and completeness. There was, sometimes, a feeling of being part of a whole. The group of people, brothers, sisters and a mom and a dad, gave me my first taste of a curious kind of love. The whole of us, as long as we stayed whole, were held together with an unspoken, unexpressed and silent stitching that held tightly the fabric of our existence. Take away one person, and the fabric ripped and weakened our sense of Family. The whole of it was fragile, thin, and worn in areas damaged by our unspoken and held-back words of love and support and appreciation of each other. We never said the words.

Children learn from their parents, and we had poor teachers. We had little example of what love was as we grew inside this pod of a Family. Father had never learned what it was, nor how to properly express it, or to sustain it. Mother strained all of her life to have it, but never felt she possessed it in the way she needed. All six of their children strained and struggled to confirm its existence in each of our own lives, but only found it when we managed to do some kindness for someone else. We were never much fed on a steady diet of love, but much more learned of it, as we cared for one another, drawing tightly by our need for one another at times. When we didn't care, when we ignored and neglected each other, love did not exist, and did not guide our decisions, and did not influence our choices for the better. On these occasions, we were starved for love.

The expression of love, as I mentioned, did not find purchase in so many words. It came in silence, finding its way in small and unassuming ways: a touch, a stroke of the hair, permission to use another's possessions, or play with someone else's toy.

For Father, expressions of love came through food. He worked several years in restaurants, apprenticing and learning the art of cuisine and embracing the culinary arts. As his expertise and professional prowess grew, he created great feasts and dishes never to be equaled. We returned his love, with great praises and the show of unabashed begging for more of his specialty dishes. Broccoli and beef stir-fry or his prime rib feast was the ultimate goal of love we sought from his hands throughout our lives, and whenever our lives came together as adults.

Another avenue of love came from Dad through play. He was a Peter Pan, and never grew tired of playing on a level children could understand. A lack of money never prevented him from taking his children to parks and playing with us for hours. He made and flew kites, splashed in ocean water at nearby beaches, teased and chased, and we chased him.

Mother's love was more difficult to find, to receive, to experience. She did not want to be a mother in life, and with six children, and eight pregnancies, she found herself trapped by the tangled coils of marriage, sex and unwanted pregnancies that left her dry, drained and bereft of the life she thought she deserved. She complained bitterly that all the pregnancies robbed her of all the calcium and minerals her body needed. She lost her pretty, large white teeth; she suffered when they rotted and were pulled out. She was depressed. She embraced her illnesses and found the author of her aches and pains in the fact that she had so many children. Her suffering in life was inextricably tied to each of our births. Yet, the house, the noise of kids, the television. and the comfort of food, anesthetized her into feeling secure, if not resigned, to the world of responsibilities that befell her as a mother and a wife. This was it for her. No other place for her to go, and no other chance for love to come in other forms. Quite simply, this was the life she chose. How many women in the 1950's felt this very same way: trapped and uninspired as a home-bound wife and mother?

Yet, I would learn later in life that the real truth of her pain and suffering emanated from the secrets she (and Dad) kept about their marital past.

The one compensation for such a lousy life was that mom could laugh, in fact, loved to laugh. We knew how to make Mother laugh, and when she did, our hearts leapt, and the mother-child bond encircled us all too briefly, and sometimes lasted only as long as her smile. Ironically, as she grew older, Mother took great comfort in having her six children around her, like chicks under *the feathers of a mother hen. She may not have liked motherhood, but I believe she loved her brood.*

Together, we acknowledged our roles as sister or brother, son and daughter, and recognized mother and father at the head of our family. We managed to grow together in the small, tight and dirty confines of our little tract house. We gave a reluctant respect to a father who thought respect was demanded and required more than earned and freely given. We skirted gingerly around our mother as she grew more and more reliant on the medical community to provide her with compassion, strength and attention. And we grew up. As we grew, we discovered that nothing we ever did really affected the other. We made decisions that took us away from each other, until our choices created a new life, and we moved away and moved on. Careers, marriages, schooling and the pursuit of love and happiness due to us all carved paths that led away from the nest we knew as children. Each path led away from what we knew as home, and each path took us away from each other.

Finally, as inevitable as death is, we gathered twice more as a Family to bury first the father, and then the mother who reluctantly gave us life, and with them, we buried the tattered legacy of love as we knew it. With their loss, the remnant of us struggled with the torn patchwork of the fabric of our love, each taking a piece called memory and walking away. Love contains this pathos, this sadness and failed to hold a group of people together. The stitches that were Mom and Dad were removed, and the family flew apart.

But here's the thing: somewhere in this watery, dismal portrait of a family is a real love story. I am referring to real, genuine, deep and abiding love that holds a man to one woman for life. Most of us can only hope love endures in our lives, but here, in this story, covered in layers of life, and nearly smothered to extinction from the weight of it, was a deep and abiding love that survived despite all attempts to ruin it or undo it. It is a love story that defies everyone's attempt to stamp it out, to ignore it, to pretend it didn't exist. It is a beautiful love story, and it was my mom and dad's story. It's the story of David and Laura, and it needs to be told. And you won't know how you "feel" until you know their whole story.

Now, here is where "fact meets fiction." I think I know their story from bits and pieces gleaned from my childhood memories, but in truth, while I know all of what you are about to read is based on actual things that happened to my parents, it all happened before I was born. Obviously, conversations, incidents and even characterizations of all the characters, including my own parents, are subject to fictional dramatization because no one now alive can corroborate the real story of how these events actually happened. In my own opinion as the author, it would not be a stretch of the imagination to characterize the level of racial prejudice that surrounded my parents in 1945. And as their daughter, what happened to my parents was beyond measure, and clearly an ugly, underhanded and treacherous act of betrayal and hatred.

Chapter 1

Harry was a scheming man, born to manipulate and determined to get his way. He knew at an early age that he was neither a handsome man, nor a man of much charm. People did not ordinarily respond to him because of who he was, so he learned to make demands of others because of what he was. And what he was, at least in his homeland of China, was a feudal lord. He was a wealthy landowner, and this alone, brought respect, attention, devotion and to some degree an idolatry that gave him what he needed: power over others.

It was not always so, and his beginnings were humble, his parents' poor, his village destroyed by neighboring warlords. As a youth, he drifted between villages, always in search of food and a place to rest. He was not especially hard-working but found it easier to steal and gain what he needed from others by his wits alone. He left his poor family behind to follow a warlord's camp for a season. Here, amongst thieves and soldiers, he discovered how much more profitable it was to simply take what you needed or wanted by force and make it your own. People, he learned, rarely fought back, even when a village far outnumbered his small band of robbers. It was the threat and the show of bravado and bluff that made others cower and turn over their food and possessions to satisfy the larceny of his forceful comrades.

Harry grew up learning how to be powerful, how to trick others into kowtowing, how to gain what others had for himself, and he learned that money was everything. China's warlords were simply men who had the vision and foresight to take what others had and make it their own – this gave them ruling power over others.

Unfortunately for Harry, he could not keep his hands off the plunder of another, and he was forced to flee for his life on several occasions.

Not being able to camp with powerful warlords, and for his own safety, he drifted ever inland away from the influences of other powerful men, and found himself smaller prey in villages far, far inside the vast and easterly plains of China's lowlands. The further away from civilization he traveled, the less those villages were prepared again predators, and the easier it was for Harry to manipulate these poor farmers into giving him what he wanted. It was so easy.

He had also stolen a formidable warlord's uniform with braids and bold armor, as well as the silk robes of a nobleman. With these disguises, he could pose in any manner of personalities, from a military man to a well-funded landowner. With promises to reimburse others who devoted their time and money, food and hospitality on him, he would move quickly and swiftly through the small villages and the unsuspecting and far-too-amiable villagers. In exchange for a good meal, a place to sleep and the good company of those wishing to impress him, all he had to do was recount war stories and tales of city life which were so foreign and exciting to these simple country folks. It suddenly occurred to him that if he played out the role of a nobleman with money, he could dupe these same simple country people into relieving them of their properties altogether. It gave him considerable sleepless nights thinking of how he could elevate his own position under the very eyes of these unsuspecting foolish people.

He stole away in the middle of the night from a village that catered excessively to his needs. He had decided to put some distance between the villages that knew him and travel east far away from the roads, towns and places he had already enjoyed. If his plan was to work, he needed to be where no one knew him, and where a new subterfuge could be perpetrated without fear of discovery.

He traveled for days, crossing the paths of others who traveled west, until he had traveled without seeing anyone at all for some miles. The fields changed, and he passed a singular and difficult mountain range to arrive at new valleys stretched far below him. Though he had no map and was uncertain where he was, he had come to several hundred miles of the border of India. The concept of another country being so close to him did not register. What did he know of the world outside of his own? The roads he traveled were not on traditional trade routes. The fact that he did not see another living soul for days meant that any village he would come upon would, indeed, be isolated.

In another two days journey, he was nearly at the base of the mountains, just above the valleys below. From his vista, he could see two, maybe three distinct villages, small, but where fire lights glowed, and people obviously lived. He camped near some caves above these villages to give himself time to think and prepare. On the evening of the second night and realized he needed a horse.

Deciding his plan was worth the effort, Harry made his way back to civilization. He returned the same way he had come, marking landmarks along the way that would lead him precisely back to the cave he just left. Making sure he stayed on well-traveled roads; he sought a proper horse that met his needs. In a few days, he came upon what he needed. A small group of travelers were encamped. From their fire, Harry could make out three horses tied to trees several yards away from the groups. Two horses were obviously pack horses, and one was a very fine mount indeed. The horse had a fine leather and wooden saddle; it was muscular and handsome. The horse was befitting a nobleman. He had found what he needed. He waited in the shadows.

Night fell, darkness descended, and the campfire died down to embers. All in camp slept. Harry carefully made his way to the tethered horses, and laid bundles of sweet grass before each as he stroked their shanks. As the horses settled into their late-night snack, Harry wrapped the feet of his intended with cloth and rope. With a handful of grass, he led the horse slowly and quietly away from the encampment. When he and the horse had traveled on foot for an hour, he removed the cloth from the horse's hooves, mounted the horse and rode quite literally like a mad man until early morning of the next day. He and the horse hid by day, and traveled only at night, covering their tracks using a branch of a tree tied to the horse's tail. On the seventh day, he came upon the caves again where he had left his meager belongings. Here he rested, eating fish from the nearby stream, feeding his horse inside the cave, and making sure no one could see his fire at night.

For several days, Harry worked with the horse so that it recognized his new owner, knew his smell, and did not flinch in his presence. He trained the horse tenderly to come to him, to obey him, and bond with him to ensure a loyalty he needed to complete his ruse. When he felt ready, he cleaned himself well, washing his horse and brushing him with straw until he shone. He changed into the warlord's uniform, prepared his long hair into a fashionable topknot (he knew how most powerful men wore their hair) held in place by a leather strap around his forehead, and tucked a small, intricately carved box inside his top armor. Inside this box was a small scroll prepared by a high commissioned teacher, indicating great power and wealth bestowed upon a certain warlord Harry worked briefly for. He overheard conversations with the Warlord soldiers that the man had a treasure box he kept close to himself. It was rumored to contain a piece of paper giving the Warlord power and authority over land to rule over several villages. Harry never saw the box or scroll to confirm its contents; he only knew he wanted what the warlord had: the power to rule over others. He watched carefully, and saw the little box carried away in the hands of the Warlord several times. He was patient, and one day the Warlord announced that he and several soldiers would ride ahead to scout for lucrative villages to pillage and would return in three days. Here was his opportunity.

When no one was looking, Harry sneaked into the tent of his master. After careful and quiet probing, the box was found under a pile of robes. Stuffing the box into his tucked in shirt Harry ran off with it the dead of night. Nobody knew, nobody missed him. When the warlord came back, Harry wasn't even suggested as the possible thief. No one knew him and did not feel his absence.

He would use this box, should anyone demand evidence of his right to claim their land, or if anyone was smart enough to demand to read documentation. Harry rode toward the greater lights of the two most visible villages below.

The effect was stunning and showy, and just has he had planned. The still of their quiet evening was shattered as Harry rode in hard, bringing his galloping horse to a powerful stop, letting the horse dance in front of the screaming and terrified village. It seemed like an invasion, and their frightened eyes rapidly scanned their fields for other marauders.

"Who is in charge here?" bellowed Harry. A simple-clothed and older man came forward and kowtowed at the ground in front of him.

"You will give me lodging and food this night, and you will be rewarded for your efforts to please me." Making sure they had little time to think, he continued to issue orders. "You there. Tend to my horse and see that he is well-fed and watered."

"Sir, sir! Good sir. Have you and your army come to destroy us?" asked the cowering man whose face was firmly planted in the earth.

"Be at peace, all who are here," Harry shouted. "I have not come to destroy you, but to make you mine." He dismounted in a haughty fashion, watching their unbelieving eyes transfixed upon him. "So far, so good," he thought to himself as he headed for the simple house in front of him. Every soul bowed low to the ground as he went through the small crowd of very simple country folk.

The villagers made no resistance to this quick and absolute takeover. Suddenly their land became my grandfather's land, and he their feudal landlord. All they did was in his honor, and for his benefit. The wife he took a year later was freely given from among their choicest virgins. Her beauty satisfied his plans, and she conquered her fear and learned the rules of ruling with might, fear and imposition. The years that mounted up brought on an apathy and boredom, and as rumors of foreign travel made their way through his little dominion, Harry grew impatient for new opportunities for gain.

Harry was my grandfather – or the man who took my father as his own. He took these two small villages, and created his own dynasty, just as he took the life of my father for his own purposes, raising him up as another soldier in his selfish cause of power and greed. He was adopted by us as much as our father was adopted by Harry.

Once landing in this country, he dispensed with his old ways. Harry was eager to assimilate into this new world called America.

Tongs were organizations based on geographical "clans" in China. You belong to the Tong that spoke your dialect, knew your village and had a relationship with your kinsmen. A Tong was responsible for sponsoring you and keeping track of you while in America. Harry's Tong taught him the basics of setting up businesses, and he became familiar with licenses and the approval of local governments to operate only the specific businesses that were allowed under the laws of the land. As Chinese immigrants, they could be employed as day laborers, still referred to as "coolie" work. They could operate some small storefronts, laundry houses, restaurants, shoeshine and shoe repair and cater to the trade needs of their own people within the confines of those areas designated as "China" towns. Two existed in the San Francisco Bay area, one between Stockton and Grant Avenues, running approximately twelve square blocks, and a smaller, more confined neighborhood across the Bay in Oakland.

Although Harry familiarized himself, and taught his sons, the laws of the land, and how to operate under them without attracting attention, he grew contemptuous of all these rules. He was a self-governing man. He was used to ruling, not being ruled by the "fees" and "taxes" levied on the Chinese immigrants. It rankled him beyond irritation. What satisfied him, for the moment, was planning how to gain the most from what he was able to do under the confines of these man-made rules. It mattered not whether these businesses operated in White neighborhoods, or in Chinatowns, although Harry acknowledged that prosperity and run-ins with the governing Law would best be avoided if he operated businesses that catered to his own kind, within the confines of prescribed Chinatown boundaries. To operate outside these confines only invited trouble and attracted too much attention from locals whose prejudices convinced them these yellow heathens were here to take jobs away from them, and food from their own families' mouths. Yellow, slanty-eyed foreigners could never be trusted.

So, gathering his five sons together, he planned. He figured the best way to profit would be to send each son to a major city, where need demanded services, and services demanded money. The more operations he could establish, the more money he could potentially gain, and any fool, especially immigrants coming to this great land, knew money was the means for every success. Money was the Gold Mountain.

He chose Chinese territories in Sacramento, Los Angeles, San Francisco, New York and Chicago, and bound with strict instructions, and seed money, Harry sent his five sons out to conquer this land. He stayed close to the youngest boy, Jimmy, to guide him and control the other brothers. Jimmy was their prize, their prince, and all four brothers were protective of their little brother. Using this to his advantage, Harry made sure Jimmy never left his side. Each were bound to their father to send a specific percentage of their wages and earnings, and in turn, Harry paid their business fees, licenses and taxes. Each understood, the more money earned, the greater the profits after all else was paid. Expansion was encouraged, but well-controlled by Harry from his principality in San Francisco where he ruled from a small apartment over a Chinese restaurant. He stayed ensconced in this relative hovel, until the San Francisco police arrested him for operating an illegal gambling house and a house of ill-repute.

Of course, Harry saw real money potential in the exploitation of his own people. Again, for him, it was easy. San Francisco held a myriad of opportunities, but the majority of "coolie" work was menial and the wages far too low to make it profitable. He could barely make more than the coolie that did all the labor. Looking around him, surveying all the possibilities, Harry found that the heart of man could be swayed by vice. Vice meant liquor, gambling and women. The weaknesses of the flesh were where he could count on every man to spend what little wages he earned. It was all too easy.

He, of course, was not the first to think of this, and in San Francisco there existed several houses of ill-repute and several back-street gambling dens where liquor flowed like piss on the streets. His first mistake was in not sharing. In his greed, Harry failed to provide the fine police of San Francisco with their fair share. Hoping to operate discreetly by moving his "dens" around the city, he was caught and jailed.

Operating on the existing but obscure laws at the time, including the 1870 California laws preventing prostitution by "Chinese", "Japanese", and "Mongoloid" women, as well as the old Chinese Exclusion Act, which detailed the exporting of Chinese "criminals", Harry faced possible confinement for one year, and deportation at the end of his prison sentence. The rules of local government cemented the hatred he had for all Gwailo.

If it weren't for the White attorney paid for by his Chinese Tong, and the $5,000 cash he donated to his Tong brothers, Harry would have been flung far from the shores of this money land he grew so fond of. His only promise made before the court was to leave San Francisco, leave the judge the $5,000, and not return for a period of ten years.

Harry took Jimmy and headed south to the sleepy farming

community known as Salinas, California. Here, Harry re-established his presence in the small Chinese community, and quickly learned their needs in order that he could convert that knowledge in a lucrative business for himself. This time, however, Harry was wise to acquaint himself with the local law enforcement, and from this a beneficial business arrangement was born. Salinas, at the time, had one Sheriff and two deputies. The Gwailo here were more simple-minded and more easily manipulated. All three were on his payroll, and from that advantage, Harry quickly set about arranging for another gambling house that offered women and liquor for all those who had money to spend. What was theirs truly, once again, became his with which he ruled with a greedy closed fist. The agreement with the local law was to stay within the blocks confined to Chinese only and to prevent criminal mischief in any of the streets of the town. What the sheriff did not acknowledge went on in his town, he could not be offended by. Since most town folks stayed away from the small Chinese enclave at night, they also did not know what went on at night. Harry finally found his quiet niche in yet another remote village.

Yet Harry could not help but feel contempt at the White rules and laws that reminded him that he held no real power in this country. That despite any attempts at wealth, real money could not be made freely under the constraints of this prejudicial white world. He could not thoroughly dominate, and that irked him. His foray into this foreign land proved to him that he might still rule over his lesser brethren and countrymen, but he clearly could not contend or even be considered on a level playing field with the White man: even the ones that he paid to look the other way. He had to be gentle with them. He had to exercise patience. Worse, he had to "kowtow" to perpetuate the myth that they ruled over him. The act, and indeed, it was an act, left galling bitterness in his throat. He hated it. He hated all White people and considered his white lords to be inferior to him. "Gwailo!" He spat. They knew nothing of real rule, worthy rule, and did not deserve his equal respect.

The only thing left for Harry was to act like it did not matter. He acted well in his outward approach to Salinas' fair-haired Sheriff and his two lumbering deputies. Harry grinned, bowed and showed his teeth in politeness whenever these men came into his restaurant. And they came in frequently, not only for their monthly pay, but they loved his Chinese food, which was laid out before them free of charge in a banquet style. Here, Harry excelled at his acting, and in return and at the same time, he got his revenge.

His restaurant staff were trained to always invite his special "guests" to the back dining room, where they could dine away from the frequenting crowds of customers held out front. In the "back" room, Harry would attend to his special "guests" himself, always with a great smile, eagerness, attentiveness and a polished flourish aimed to please. Knowing these three White men always ordered the same "house" Chow Mein, deep-fried shrimp and Chinese ribs, Harry instructed his staff to prepare what became known as the "Sheriff Special." The revenge came in the cooking.

With skill and acumen, the two kitchen cooks stir-fried the food, picking up their seasonings with long-handled metal spoons, and oils and sauces, as gas flames flared under their busy woks on the hot commercial kitchen stove. Once the noodles and meat were plated, the cooks would unzip their pants and proceed to urinate onto the three plates of chow mien. Others held a finger to the outside of their nostril and blew chunks of nasal matter into the plates. A final stir and a quick flourish of soy sauce and onions hid the "special" ingredients from the unsuspecting and under-educated palates of Harry's special guests. Harry would dance before the cart of food as it was wheeled before his happy and very eager customers. The kitchen staff smiled happily. His beautiful waitresses grinned and were instructed to brush their breasts against these white "devils" as they set down their plates.

The Sheriff always praised Harry, insisting almost every time, "Damnit, Harry. I don't know what you put into your food, but man, this stuff can't be beat!"

Harry would grin and nod in return as he watched them eat. His joy was very genuine as he bowed low several times and told them to "Eat!" "Eat!"

Chapter 2

China and its political and social structures are ancient, complicated, and history would bear witness to how messed up it became. In the 19th Century, while Queen Victoria enjoyed the "Golden Age of Man" and the Victorian Upper Class ruled Society like a wet wool robe that chaffed and smelled like wet dog, China was experiencing extreme internal turmoil.

China, it seemed, was unable to rule anything it called its own. Powerful nations wanted to exploit every opportunity to profit from Chinese opium. Indeed, opium trade resulted in two trade wars between China and Britain, and their second European war involved both Britain and France. The problems that opium caused China were unending, and every attempt by the Chinese ruling class to disrupt or disband, burn, kill and cripple opium trade was met with debilitating resistance and eventual failure. There simply was too much profit to be made from this drug trafficking to end the cash crop. The British intended to keep the trade of opium open and sent their military to prevent any Chinese governing element from blocking opium shipping from Canton's harbor.

The conflict, in which the British were victorious, resulted in the Treaty of Nanjing. The treaty provided for specific concessions by the Chinese government. An already poor country ripped apart by its own warlords, drug lords, and attacks from bordering lands, China was made to pay for their feeble attempts to prohibit opium trade. It cost them an unbelievable 21 million dollars, and they were forced to cede five major shipping ports for British trade, commerce and residence. It included the right of British citizens living in China to be tried for any offense only in British courts. It was during this Treaty that Britain gained control over Hong Kong and its harbors.

Already made vulnerable and weak by the powerful British, China stepped into deeper humiliation. In October 1856, Canton police acting on observation and tips provided by local dock workers, boarded a British-registered ship called *The Arrow*, docked in Canton harbor. The ship and its crew were arrested for various crimes of smuggling. This unpopular incident led to the second 'war' with Great Britain. The British involved France, and the Anglo-French alliance invaded the city of Canton creating a barricade of wills against the local Chinese. No trade was allowed in or out of this busy port. Broken by their occupation, China entered the Treaty of Tianjim in 1858, yielding more ports to British occupation and rule and allowing foreign emissaries, and Christian missionaries freedom of movement throughout China's interior. China had become whipped and, for the moment, tamed by humiliation.

It was only temporary, as the Chinese government refused to ratify the 1858 Treaty. This led to an Anglo-French attack on the Emperor's Summer Palace. Having suffered yet another ignominious defeat, China signed the Convention of Peking, and promised to observe and obey the Treaty's conditions.

Too weak to oppose, and made defenseless by their own internal troubles, China became Britain's eastern footstool. Between 1850 and 1873 the Taiping Rebellion caused an insurmountable loss of Chinese and local life, estimated to be between 20 and 30 million people and involving 17 provinces at war with each other. This internal war stripped the Ch'ing Dynasty of most of its ruling force and political power. Their own devastation left them a weak opponent of rising and imposing European occupation. It was easy to strip a dying dragon of its wealth and opportunity as it made no resistance because of its vulnerability, China was ripe for yet another revolution.

The ripened revolutionary leadership came from Canton's own countryside. Revered as the "Father of modern China," Sun Yat-sen was born in southern Guangdong Province, educated in Hawaii, and had a short career as a medical doctor before turning his attention to politics and Chinese government reform. As yet, still unpopular, Sun Yat-sen formed a secret society for Chinese reform while living in exile in Japan. He brought together several revolutionary groups to form the Revolutionary Alliance Society whose program is the now "famous "Three People's Principles of Nationalism." It demanded freeing all of China from foreign control, instilling democracy, overthrowing the current Manchu Dynasty and introducing a democratic political system. His revolutionary spirit swept through China, especially catching the energy of youthful students and even soldiers.

In the summer of 1900 members of this secret society roamed throughout northeastern China. Bands of these revolutionaries killed Europeans and Americans. Buildings owned by *Feng Quay* or "White ghosts" were burned and destroyed. These bands of young revolutionaries called themselves I-ho ch'uan, or "Righteous and Harmonious Fists." They practiced a kind of martial art that had boxing elements to it, and its practice was thought to make them impervious to bullets. The world press reported this uprising as the Boxer Rebellion, and called its members simply, Boxers.

The weakened Ch'ing Dynasty took this opportunity to ally

themselves with The Boxers, (anything to rid its country of outsiders.) European businessmen, American traders, Christian missionaries were all targets, and yet The Boxers failed to drive the foreign devils out of China. Unsuccessful in establishing himself as a ruling government, Sun left Japan to set up a new separate Chinese government, installing himself as 'generalissimo' of a new regime in 1923.

Having allied himself with the Soviet Union, Sun Yat-sen modeled his party after the Soviet Communist Party, and appointed Chiang Kai-shek as its president. Sun's Three Principles of the People 'platform united a great deal of China under its political philosophy of nationalism, democracy and socialism.

In 1920, somewhere in the Canton provinces of Southern China, my Father was born. At the same time, Sun's followers formed the Comintern, also known as the Communist International. They slowly and surreptitiously formed small communist groups, printed and disseminated huge amounts of pamphlets and other printed materials to anyone who could read, and started a grass roots movement that began to spread in popularity. One such member was Mao Zedong. A meeting in Shanghai in 1921, in which the young Mao was present, formed the first party congress to be known as the Communist Party of China, or the CCP.

It wasn't until my father entered the world of this China, that things suddenly got more interesting.

Chapter 3
Meet my father.

My father was a Pan. Like Peter, he did not want to grow up. He retained a perpetual fondness for fun, laughter and mischievousness. He was born in China. Rumor has it he was born in a "City" because of his accent but raised in the "country" where he learned a country dialect of Cantonese rather than the "City" dialects of Mandarin. We were told somewhere in the far western provinces of Guangdong Provence is where his real Family sold our father as a young baby to a wealthy Landowner bearing the village name of Yee. The Yee Family, or Yee Village, had a bit of wealth and privilege far from the influence and oversight of any Chinese provisional government. The Yee village existed, like many, without overlords, military occupation or any Christian influences for many long years. And yes, I said he was sold. The sale of children is of no great revelation, especially for China, but what was unusual was the sale of a baby boy. A male child, in Chinese society, is highly prized, and female babies are considered a poor substitute. Girls were readily sold, hired out for work, slavery or abandonment, or even worse, drowned for their worthlessness. But a boy! There was your prize, your blessing, your hopes for your future. So, why was he sold to the Yee Family? We do not know. My Father never knew why, and like many "adopted" people, he grew up with a great longing to know his real parents. Two stories resulted from his search, both stories offered some comfort, perhaps both stories were meant only to comfort and assuage the pain of the loss he felt. The one story was that they were so poor and wanted for food and money, they had no choice but to sell him to the Yees'. The other story was that the Yee Family was desirous of helping my father's family, and promised they would provide not only for the boy's education, but would eventually send him to the United States, where he would surely prosper in the Gold Mountain. The mere mention of the Gold Mountain in those lean days of China's history meant untold wealth and prosperity to all Chinese. It was a golden ticket to a golden opportunity, one which could not be ignored, and so he was sold, or given up, or handed over to the Yee Family in a moment of great sacrifice and utter hope for his future. He remembered having a father, a mother, and two twin sisters, obviously older than him. Knowing how valuable sons were, why was he sold and not his sisters? It made him feel unwanted, rejected and somehow, he felt, his fault, as though he had to be given up, so their lives could go on. He asked many times when he was growing up with the Yee's, "Why did they give me up?" "Why was I sold, and not my sisters?" And so, the stories grew in order to quiet his feelings, and most certainly to avoid telling him any truths. It was a terrible thing. He knew the stories they told him were not true, and each time he sought the truth, they served him a package of intentional lies. He stopped asking at one point, never having satisfied his itch for the truth. The Yee Family, as he grew to know them, were not only unreliable, unconcerned and dismissive of him, but they would turn out to be his biggest and most damaging enemy. Dad's life circled these people for much of his youth. He had to. He not only belonged to them, but because of indebtedness for bringing him to the United States, he was intentionally indentured and required to pay them back for all their efforts. Because he made so very little in wages, my father knew he would be "tied" to the Yee's for a long time. Perhaps forever.

Father came over with several other boys of various ages. The Yee Family was comprised of Father Harry Yee, and his five adult sons: Jimmy, Shorty, Sam, Frank and Joey. These were their chosen American names. Several years before my father was acquired, Harry and his five sons left their village, leaving their mother (and Harry's wife) in charge as "Landlord". They became émigrés to America, seeking out their collective fortunes, and (initially) sending money or gold and silver back to China to enhance their influence and financial strength in their village. Each son was sent to Chinatowns across the country, and after establishing laundry houses and restaurant businesses, each had instructions to send a majority percentage of their incomes to Harry for safe keeping, and live on as little as they needed to get by after paying their debts. The plan was that Harry would invest their funds in his hidden businesses of prostitution and local underground gambling, sending home money periodically to satisfy his wife in China. Harry was a hard-handed father and his sons learned over the years, never to cross him, cheat him of money or lie to him at pain of punishment, which sometimes could be severe.

Chapter 4

The story goes like this: The Dragon was starving. China, for all its millions after millions of people and for its grand land mass had been conquered and beaten by so many external and internal political machinations, there was little breath left to defend the dragon. So, it was left to starve. The strength of China did not lie in the hands of its government, nor did her power wield a wide circle of influence from inside the Forbidden City. The strength in China belonged to those who still owned land and to the people who tilled the soil.

Well beyond the gentrified cities and the southern rural province of Quandong (once known as Canton) were many small and very remote villages. Far to the west of the cities by the China Sea were the delta farm lands and fields open and ripe with agriculture and rural life way toward the west approaching the backside of the Himalayan mountains. One village was heard to be rich and prosperous. It lay close to the feet of India's Himalayan mountains.

In the heart of this vast rural country life sat a brittle and cold old woman. She was the village's Matriarch who ruled with an iron will though her fists were small and crippled with age. She sat imperious, as though she were the lady dowager of an undeclared royal line. She ruled from her handsomely hand-carved teak chair overlooking a beautiful rural farmland terraced in planted rice, fruits and vegetables. She owned twenty thousand hectares of rich land and on it all the people who worked it for her.

From her modest hilltop home of brick and wood, she could survey her kingdom from the open veranda, indeed, from any side of her house she was able to step on to her balconies and survey all she owned. Her cunning but cataract eyes took great pleasure in watching the daily chores of those who worked for her. Her land contained three villages. Hers was a fiefdom. Those who tilled and harvested from her soil were her servants, and though they were able to eat off her land, live in modest huts, and even earn wages that she dictated, she was feudal mistress of them all. The daily hum and hue of her well-cared for land was a demonstration of wealth and prosperity in an otherwise dying country. Here, in the far southwestern countryside, news of the outside was rare, and her land remained in her pristine control with no fear or threat of big city hostilities finding their way into her garden.

Far removed from the Dragon which lay starving beyond her borders, the Matriarch felt impervious and invincible. She had storehouses of food, fruits, fresh, dried and pickled vegetables and all manner of oxen, pigs and goats. Those who served her enjoyed huts of straw and mud. Groups of ten shared their meals around hammered woks and clay and metal pots. Several small villages dotted her landscape where whole families flourished on her land. They worked hard during the day but were rewarded with full bellies at night and a shelter they could call home.

So prosperous was her rice and the fruits from her soil that rumors found their way to the ears of others outside much like the smell of roasting pig to the noses of those who had not eaten for a long while. Like many poor, indigent farmers trying to find a way to feed their families and stay alive, my 'father's real father moved south-east, away from the dying and warring cities and towns to find a new life.

It was 1922, and my father was now two years old, still strapped tightly to his mother's back. The first Communist Party meeting was held in Shanghai the year before, and a new attitude toward communism was beginning to plant seeds in the faraway cities of China. As my father's father moved his family along unfamiliar roads alongside creek beds, his only thought was how to survive. He pushed a wooden wheelbarrow cart that held their few belongings: some cooking utensils, clothing that doubled as bedding, a small bag of rice, a bit of salted pork and some pickled preserves in a clay pot. His wife carried my father on her back, and her two twin daughters, now seven years old, walked behind their parents. They had been walking and camping for ten days now, and were weary enough that they plodded in silence, their eyes concentrating on the placement of their feet, one step after another. Sometimes the children hopped onto the wheelbarrow when their father felt strong enough. Other times, the father took the baby, and the mother pushed the cart forward

. It was in the small town of Shin-Tzou that a man took pity on the poor family huddled under the tin eve of a closed storefront they had hastily run under as the rain poured down on them. He motioned to them to come into his home, and there they dried out in front of his fire, and gratefully ate of his humble broth and rice. Shin-Tzou was dying too, the man told them. He was a teacher and leaving himself for Canton near the coast. The influences of Sun Yat-Sen were being felt in the southern province of Guangdong, and the teacher wanted to hear more of his political agenda. He taught Confucianism in school but felt enervated by the words of this much-admired and seemingly popular leader. He invited my Father's Father and his family to join him, promising good jobs in the big city. My grandfather nodded, not wishing to offend, and told the Teacher he was but a humble tiller of the earth, and he needed to farm. To be courteous and respectful, the Teacher told him of a prosperous village in the most rural and southern part of China where a kindly old matriarch let people farm her land and live in harmony with her. It was many days travel because it was so far removed from towns and cities, but he gave the best directions he could, and offered them a small sack of rice and some preserves. They slept by his kitchen fire, and in the morning parted their ways.

Many days later, now down to a small handful of rice, my grandfather began to consider this venture folly, when in the distance, he saw a man herding four oxen that pulled a long cart covered in oilcloth. There was a boy of about ten who sat astride the lead ox. He approached, grateful to let go of the wheelbarrow long enough to talk to the man. Had he heard of the matriarch's village? The man took his long willowy stick which he used to prod the beasts' backsides, and arched it high over his head, pointing it as last to the road behind him. Once over the hill they were but twenty-eight miles from her village. Certain their long and painful journey was now ending, they stopped for the night, camping near the creek they had been following for days. Grandfather played with his son, my father, while his mother prepared the last of their food. *"It does not matter, because tomorrow we will be taken in by this benevolent old woman, given our own land and a chance to prosper again,"* thought grandfather. My father's real family lay on a spot of earth in the southwestern-most province of rural China with dreams of escaping the hungry Dragon one last time.

In the early dawn, while my father still slept cradled in swaddling, his father, mother and two sisters rose, took up their meager belongings and headed for the crest of the far-off hill. The road rose and fell away, one after the other, until as the sun sat low and heavy in the western sky, grandfather dropped the cart at the top of the last conquered hill and looked out on the valley below. Several huts dotted a beautifully groomed and pleasant garden valley. Rows of fruit trees edged rows of vegetables on the valley floor. Pens of pigs and oxen and goats were handsomely stabled to the left and right of the huts that were aligned randomly five here, three there. The valley rose to terraced rice fields hugging the foothills, there watered pools shimmered in the glow of the setting sun. It was so gold and green! High above the rice paddies sat an impressive but small wooden house, with a veranda that encircled the structure on all sides. The craftsmanship of the teak railing and the green and gold tiles of the roof glinting in the setting sun made it obvious who lived there. People were now looking up and pointing at them, as they headed down the last slope of their journey.

They walked into the village proper just as the sun fell behind the western mountain. Wang Chow was the first to come forward and greet the travelers. He motioned them to sit around the fire pit, as an older woman and a younger woman offered them water from clay jars. The mother gratefully took my two-year-old father from her weary back, and plopped him down between her feet as she raised the jar to her parched lips. He gnawed at the jade baby bracelet on his tiny wrist, amused by his own drooling.

"Even the water is sweet here," thought grandfather. "How may one be allowed to farm here?" my grandfather asked while wiping his lips.

"Oh, you must see the Matriarch," Wang Chow answered, his eyes motioning up the hillside. "She will not see you now, it is too late in the day. But enjoy our fire, rest, eat with us. Our food we gladly share in exchange for stories of your adventures," he proffered. "We much enjoy tales from far off places and cities we know little of," he clarified. Grandfather felt at home with people of his kind. They understood the earth, and the earth held no secrets from them. Several others, mostly women and young girls came forward and greeted the strangers, and bringing their own pots, joined the others in making a small communal feast that made his mother's eyes well up with silent tears. So much food! As several young girls played delightedly with the baby boy, and two girls who looked like mirror images of themselves, their mother helped the women prepare the food in flashes of chopping and stir-frying, the air was soon pungent with the aroma of good food. Rice cooked in a large earthen pot stuck in the ground, its lid just above the earth, and was tended to all day long, never empty of steamed rice.

Grandfather recounted his tale for the few men now squatting down in a circle around the fire pit, their arms casually folded over their knees, some puffing on clay pipes. He had once owned a small farm of thirty acres outside a small, but growing township. He sold his produce in town at the daily marketplace that lined the courtyard of the town. A greedy warlord from the north had swept through the town seeking to expand his territory. Within days, the local leaders were hung in the middle of the town's courtyard, and instead of a marketplace, all farmers were forced to place their produce in waiting wagons as tribute to the new Warlord. Never having met the warlord, his thugs took control of Grandfather's land, and seized his two oxen, his mule, his chickens and his small herd of goats. Their land and their animals would feed the war-monger's small army. It was when he was told to abandon his family and report as a recruit in the warlord's army that my father's father stole away in the middle of the night, family in tow, to escape conscription. Having nothing to pull his wagon, they took what they could in a small garden wheelbarrow walking in the shadows of moonless nights. Each city and town they came to seemed to be running from the pressures of politicians struggling for power and control, running from war barons determined to grab as much land as they could. Talk of Sun Yat-Sen, a Christian educated philosopher and his Nationalist Party was making grand attempts to rule China from Japan, and a new element called communism was being discussed everywhere.

There seemed no escape as cities and townships struggled against the aggressive power mongers, all who seemed to battle each other for purchase. The Boxers were still trying to eradicate foreign Christian ministries throughout China. Knowing that missionaries still populated the Southern provinces and some rural areas, rebels were spreading further and further south attempting to purge the land of their fathers from a Christian god. Townships that had already been raped, some repeatedly by opposing factions, had not survived, and he recalled for those gathered the visions of ghost towns and migrating and starving refugees like them. Everywhere they went, it seemed the landscape was scarred and left for dead.

Grandfather paused to take the first few bites of the hot and tasty meal handed him before continuing his saga. He knew he inhaled the food too quickly, as it burned the back of his throat, his chopsticks shaking in his fingers. He shoveled more slowly, chewing more deliberately with each bite. His stomach spasmed after receiving unfamiliar warmth of food.

He recalled for them places where he had found work, people he had sheltered with, and news of Nanking, Peking and Canton. He heard of a great war and how it eroded China's government further, leaving her vulnerable to foreign influences that stirred up the old boxer rebels known as the I-ho ch'uan, or "Righteous and Harmonious Fists" who wanted all foreign powers out of China.

People seemed to be migrating to the larger cities for support and refuge from land-grabbers and small armies of war lords. Farmers were frightened off, and the richness their fields once produced were plundered or left to rot and fallow in the wake of forced abandonment. Mob armies of men loaded their wagons of what they could steal, and regrouped with their generals and leaders, while others took off like thieves in the night just stealing for themselves.

The men nodded in appreciation of his story, confirming for him their own tragic stories of loss and forced exile. Some told of sons and whole families leaving for larger cities never to be heard from again. China was always changing, and its people always suffering, it seemed to them.

"But you live a rich and obviously abundant life here," countered Grandfather. "It is a beautiful village, the water is sweet, the yield of your labor is like gold," he told them. Smirks and tittering passed among their silent faces as they pondered his words. Finally, old Master Chow spoke for them declaring, "We eat and sleep from the sweat of our brows daily, but all we do is in service to Madame Yee," he said pointing to the house on the hill. We are prosperous slaves in servitude to the great landowner on the hill. She is a rich and powerful woman, and we are nothing, we have nothing, without her, and yet we make her more rich and powerful," said Chow. "This is how we prosper now," Chow told him. Grandfather thought he heard cursing under someone's breath. A man hocked and spat his phlegm into the fire.

Dinner was eagerly consumed and interspersed with chatter and the clicking of chopsticks as many exchanged, dissected, absorbed and repeated the news of what was happening outside their world. It was as tantalizing as the food itself. News gave way to gossip and speculation, and then came a gauntlet of politically partisan positions. China, it was assumed, was in the hands of the enemy, and the imperial palace in the Forbidden City no longer held power because of the infiltration and influence of foreign devils and dogs of trade. They concluded before saying good night that outsiders were responsible for the boils that took over and festered in rotting pus the once proud cities inside China's borders. Satisfied the infection could not reach them at least for this night, the fires banked, and the dishes and pots were gathered, and all turned to their own huts for the night. Master Chow invited the father of my father, and his family to sleep around the camp site outside his hut and bade them good sleep. In the morning, he would send word to the mistress on the hill that outsiders had come to seek work and a place to live.

Chapter 5

In a great show of power, the dowager gathered her workers so that they knelt on all her balconies, tightly packing themselves around her so they could listen and watch.

"More mouths to feed?" the crone's voice strained to cry aloud. "Is it I to be a servant to this world that I must use my land to feed all of you?" She raised both arms high in exclamation. The small family was kneeling, bowing, wailing and crying in front of her chair. The father prostrated himself, crawling as he cried. He reached for the lady's foot and grasped it lightly, begging her to take them in.

Madame Yee kicked his hands away in rejection. "Look how many of you! It is too much to ask. We shall all perish. No! This cannot be possible. You must leave today!" She rose from her chair to look around and made sure all eyes were upon the drama she governed.

"We will work hard for you, Venerable Lady," the father cried. "We are all strong." My father's mother was asking Buddha to help them, and with my father tied to her back, he cried with fright at the noise his Family was making. There was a pause, and the father looked up from his prone position.

"You wish to take from me," the dowager crooned. "But what will you give me in return?" Her eyes narrowed as she spoke.

"We have two girls, strong and bright to serve in your house," Grandfather replied. At this he motioned his daughters to shuffle forward on their knees. Both threw themselves forward and cried big and frightened tears.

"BAH," came the crone's reply, as she grabbed her silk robes, and turned her back on the groveling family. "My house is filled with girls. I have girls enough and I send half to other villages to marry just so I can regain some of my money from their dowries. But I never make more than I invest in these wretched creatures! More girls mean more of my time and money. There is no value for me!"

"They are twin girls, mirror images of each other. Very valuable! Very lucky!" cried the father. Again, the crowd went silent, and my family inched away from her, rejected.

In the hush of that moment, as wailing ceased and sniffles faded, my own Father's infantile crying became the only sound. The dowager turned her head slowly around.

"And this child... the baby," she queried, "is it also a girl?" She knew before she met this Family that it was not, because her counselor had told her of the newcomers to the Village.

"It is our boy, our only boy," replied the father, dropping from his kneeling position to prostrate himself at her feet.

Sensing their hesitation, the dowager barked, "Well!" "Will you not offer the boy in return for all you ask of me?"

The father looked first at his wife, as she grabbed his forearm, her eyes cast down, but her tightening grip communicating her fear. "He is our only son; seven years we waited for him."

"You presume to enter my land, ask me for my food, my lodging and my wages, and you dare offer nothing in return?" The dowager sneered, as the crowd around them murmured and whispered for the first time. A hush fell as the crone raised her hand for silence.

"You are a great and powerful Lady," Grandfather replied. "My two daughters are of great value and will work hard for you. The reason I did not drown them at birth was because they are twins. Twin girls can be sold at a higher price anywhere. They are a good sign. These girls are strong and work twice as hard. A baby boy cannot work for you, great lady."

With these words, the girls moved in unison, shuffling on their knees an inch or two closer, their faces pushed into their hands to hide their tears and fear.

"I weary of this. You waste my time. I will instruct my people to give you five days' worth of rice and some pig fat, and then you must leave us before the noonday sun." The lady sat down heavily in her chair, her eyes glazing over.

As Mother and Father looked at each other, eyes searching, the crowd moved, rustled and whispered among themselves. "Wait," the father begged. "What would you give us for the boy," he mouthed in defeat.

"Give YOU? Am I to make *you* wealthy now?" She replied.

"Madame Yee, you ask us for our only boy," the father proffered.

Choosing her words carefully, craftily, the old woman leaned into the Family quaking at her feet. "Your son shall become my son, and in return, you shall have rice and fruit, and vegetables and meat. I will exchange your rags for clothing. I will grace your palm with gold, and a letter I will provide you to the next village, instructing them to take you and your precious twin girls in. They will do as I instruct. You will be housed, clothed and fed. You will be appointed some acres of your own to plow and tend. Your girls will grow up and I will offer them in marriage, and you will prosper. You will have work for your hands to do, food in your belly at night, and a place you can call home. But you must never return to this village. You must never see your boy again. You must never come to spy on him, or ask of him again. Do you understand? Do you agree?"

The pause was palpable. Hearts beat in wild rhythms. The Father's voice filled with tears as he managed to ask, "My son, what will become of him?"

"Ha! Your son becomes mine, and he shall know my wealth and he shall grow to rule my land, and he shall inherit! She cried loudly. "You are a lucky man to have such a son. Now, I inherit *your* luck!" Her voice turned vicious in her reply, "you need not worry about your son again. In my hands, he shall rule alongside me, and when I die, he shall rule over YOU!" She looked around, seeing that all kneeling around her were appropriately horrified and frightened. She sat back and sneered, looking off into the distance.

The mother retrieved her wailing son from her back, bringing him into her arms. She held the baby tightly, fearing his absence. The father's hand went to the boy's head, and he softly stroked his son's hair. The baby's cries softened. The father and mother softly cried, their heads and their tears hovered over their baby boy; the baby's hand touched both their wet faces.

The old dowager sat imperiously. She was gratified at the feeling of such power over people. She was as good as a queen or an empress. She had power to shape people's lives anyway she chose. She was as good as a god, for their very lives were in her hands to do with as she wished. She knew their answer before it came.

"We agree," the father sighed as he spoke, wiping his face with his sleeve. The Mother crumbled on top of her toddler, her quiet tears soaking the blanket that wrapped him. She could smell that he needed changing, but for now, the smell was his, and she breathed in deeply to capture this moment in her heart. Her frightened fingers fluttered all around his body, trying to memorize what she could of him.

With these words, a small victory came over the dowager's face, and she stood and clapped her hands. "You will see to this family's needs, as I've promised. Fill their cart, clean them up and clothe them. Fill their bellies, and wait for my letter. Jinzhou, you will escort them to the village of Chou, and make certain they are received properly. Leave me, all of you. Get back to your work. This has wasted an entire morning worth of work, and I shall never regain it. Sochi, bring me my writing box." People moved and scattered away from the old woman in response.

The last to leave her were my ancestors. They silently caressed and touched their baby as tears freely flowed. But as the dowager turned and narrowed her eyes at them, they slipped their hands away from the boy and backed out of the veranda, still on their knees. The mother hid her face on both hands, as the father held her close, guiding her away from the house. Only the twin girls looked back in unison for one last glimpse of their baby brother.

As the servant girl held out the writing box on her knees, the dowager paused to move closer to the baby cooing at her feet. She bent slowly, as though her back would snap like a brittle twig, and she picked up the baby in one wobbling motion. The servant girl thought the old woman might drop the baby from her old and wizened hands. But with amazing strength, the old lady held up the child high above her head and whispered in triumphant enthusiasm. "A prince! A king! Aha! I have a treasure this day! You will be my legacy."

In truth, the old crone had five golden sons. As their lands increased, and their wealth expanded, the five sons grew bored and restless, and one day came to their aging mother with their father's plan. Each would take an equal sum and travel to the Gold Mountain. Each would go in different directions to find their fortune and return to China with honor and wealth. The son with the greatest gain would rule the others. If they failed, they would die where they were leaving instructions to send their bones home to their mother. Their mother hated the idea. After all, who would take care of her? But she was intrigued with making more money. If they sent her gold from the Gold Mountain, she could buy more land, become more powerful, and be one of the largest feudal landlords in the Southwestern Province.

So, one day, after a feast that rivaled no other, all five sons, and their notorious father bid their mother goodbye, and headed for Canton and the ship that would carry them west. Western civilization and the Gold Mountain received her five sons, and, in time, she had letters and parcels from them once each year from places such as Chicago, New York, San Francisco, and Sacramento and Los Angeles. Never having seen a map of the world, she could not envision where these strange places might be in the world, how close they might be to China, nor across what waters they might be. Her sons knew money could not be sent by packages. Any obvious attempts to send money would be instantly stolen by customs officers. Each package that arrived from each son once a year held a small container of ground spice, tightly sealed with cord and wax. When opened, and the spice poured out, the mother would find small fingerling ingots of gold shaped into thin cords each about an inch long or shorter. Here her sons had secreted her share of their wealth sent in tribute and a reminder to her of their continued success in the Gold Mountain. Now, gone twelve years, the mother secretly opened her annual packages to find the usual material, cups, plates, bits of lace and hair pins, and a single bottle of spice. At times the boxes appeared poor and sparse. But none were meaningful to her except the bottle of spice. When she poured out the bottle, sometimes only specks of gold fell out, and sometimes no gold at all. One year, one son placed a silver button with a bird symbol on it that he snipped from a soldier's uniform when he washed and pressed it. It was all the son could manage to send. The silver surprised the mother, and she cried because she felt her son's failure. As of late, the last two years, the boxes grew thin and seemingly poorly thought out. One son sent booklets with pictures and drawings and words she could not understand. The pictures showed automobiles, blonde white women with red lips and white teeth dressed in abominable clothes with animals wrapped around their shoulders. These women held cigarettes between gloved fingers, wore high silly headdresses, and their clothing showed their legs with black lines running down the backs of their legs. The magazines depicted wonders and horrors, and when she threw the magazines out her door, she was not surprised they were whisked away immediately to be devoured by each villager in turn. They were a scandalous gift. She knew, as the gold became scarce, that her sons were being swallowed up by the foreign devils that lived on the Gold Mountain, and her mighty sons were surely being victimized though they told her nothing of their adventures.

 It was beyond her power to bring her sons home, and there was still some chance of gaining more gold if they stayed where they were. But now, she was satisfied, greatly satisfied that she had a new son, another son. One that she could raise to follow her, mimic her, learn from her and one who would stay with her so that she would not die alone. The village would be his one day, and should one or more sons return alive, she would set this one over the others to punish them for abandoning her. She vowed to decry this in writing and have it publicly read aloud at the moment of her death.

As the baby began to wiggle, it was more than she could handle, so she proffered the squirming baby to her servant girl, who put down the writing box, grabbed the baby and left the room.

Pleased with having her way, the empress of a large country farm sat down to write a letter of intent to her neighbors to the north of her.

Chapter 6

My Father was now six years old and was straddling the back of a water buffalo that carried him and three other boys to and from school. It was a Confucius school taught by a local monk in the next village. Only the boys were allowed to attend school, as education was wasted on girls.

Father was happy, healthy and alive. Among these boys, and indeed the entire Yee village, he was treated with great kindness and respect. All were taught to bow to him and address him as "The One". In doing so, the dowager lady was assured that all would grow to revere him and obey his every wish, making it easier for him to transition to her level of power.

But for now, he was a youth, a child. His days were spent in the company of these three other boys whom he called friends. He was schooled, he was bathed by servants, fed by servants, and had the general run of the entire village and his surroundings. He was denied nothing. Yet, at his very heart, he was not spoiled, nor was he demanding. He loved the attention, and a genuine smile was ever-present on his small face. Although his nurse had often told him the story of how he came to the village, and how his selfish parents had sold him for money, he never felt openly sad or hurt by the story. He listened to the variety of stories whispered to him about his real family and how they came to be here. But in his heart he retained a deep hurt, a wound that never healed. *"Why did they abandon me?"*

It was on this day, coming back from school that he got off the huge back of *Tak-Tak,* the water buffalo, to run as usual, into his village. He was suddenly stopped by all the activity. Never had he seen such chaos and running around. Most days, he would return from school to find his people working methodically in the fields, bent or kneeling, the women stirring pots and the men working the soil in a serene and bucolic vista. But not today. Men ran, women screamed and yelled at one another, and ducks and chickens scattered into the air. He ran to his old Ma Ma's house on the hill.

One of the old men who worked the rice fields, ran, fell on his knees in front of the boy, as he held tightly to his small shoulders. "Run and hide, young master," he warned. "Today is not a good day."

Father struggled out of his grip his eyes focused on his Ni-Ni's house. He tore loose from the old man's grip and ran up the teak staircase. There, he saw a young man in a western suit and hat standing over his Ni-Ni, as she sat crumpled in her chair, one hand hiding her eyes. She was wailing incomprehensibly. The man spun around and eyed my father.

"So, this must be him?" he smiled. The old women wailed an octave higher than before and reached out with both arms beckoning my father to come. He ran to her arms, trembling in unison with the old woman. "You cannot," wailed the old lady.

"I have explained this all before, Mother. We need your help. We have several businesses, and if we don't get more labor, our investments will die. If they die, there will be no more gold from the Gold Mountain."

"I can give you many young girls. I can offer you brides. Cheap labor, strong labor and brides for my sons," Her voice cracked and wavered.

"And I have told you, old woman, that I cannot take females into the United States. But I can take boys!"

The old woman sobbed into the boy's small shoulder. "I shall die without a son to care for me," she moaned. "I shall die all alone."

Clearly irritated, the man walked to the edge of the veranda and leaned against the post, surveying the property. Though no maintenance was needed, several people, more than was necessary, were pretending to be busy gardening, raking and trimming bushes and flowerbeds close to the house. Their heads were down, their eyes focused on their garden tools, but their ears and even their heads inclined toward the house. The young man's face smiled and relaxed, as he reached into his suit pocket for a cigarette and lighter. He lit a curious western cigarette and inhaled.

Pausing for two more swift puffs on his cigarette, he tossed the fag to the ground; it landed close to an ancient, wrinkled man with a long white goatee. The old man bent down and picked up the cigarette and put it to his mouth. The old man grinned as he puffed and drew smoke in. Two others came to him, grabbed for the cigarette, passed it around, as all began to smoke it quickly. It emboldened the young man, as he turned to face his mother.

"Look at me, Mother," he challenged her. "Look at my clothing," he ordered her, opening his suit jacket to reveal a silk shirt against silk lining underneath. "Look at my watch. Look at this ring," he pointed each item out to her. "Are these not the riches you wanted for your sons?" "Did you not agree to send us away so that we could make great fortunes?" "Have we not been generous with our yearly packages to you?"

"Those packages do not contain what they once did. You have given me nothing lately," she reprimanded.

"Those packages show you how we are struggling to maintain our fortunes," he retorted.

"You have all this wealth and wish to get richer at my expense," she yelled back. "I spend a fortune sending my sons off to become rich men, and you still want me to sacrifice more. I cannot give you more."

The young man looked away from her, his eyes turning to the fields. He took off his white straw hat, stripped himself of his jacket and loosened his tie. "I've forgotten how hot it is here." He walked out to the veranda and took two steps down the staircase and turned to her. "I will go for a walk; perhaps I will visit the next village and see old friends. We will talk when I return." Rolling up his sleeves, he turned away and left her.

"Ni-Ni, who is he?" my father asked.

"That is your uncle," she replied wearily. "He is my youngest son, Pao Chin."

"And what does he want?" he asked her.

"To take you from me," she sniffled. Her hand flew to cover her eyes again.

"Take me where?"

"To the Gold Mountain so that you can work to make him richer," she replied bitterly.

"To the Gold Mountain," my father whispered to himself. He had heard stories around many campfires. He had seen the magazines that others had stuffed away in boxes and under their sleeping beds. He saw pictures of great stone buildings, and people who smiled from pale white faces, with strange round and pale eyes, wearing impossible clothing. *The Gold Mountain*!

"Ni-Ni! If I left, you would be sad?" he queried.

"I could not bear it, child," she told him. "Now, go and have your afternoon tea." With this, she beckoned for her servant girl to take the boy for his afternoon meal so that she could be alone to think of what to do next. The servant took the boy's hand and led him from the room. After she dried her eyes and blew her nose, her face became stone as her mind began to calculate.

Chapter 7

It was well into the evening, the stars were out, the moon was nearly at its crest, when Pao Chin returned. His shirt was opened and sweat-stained, and he now had sandals instead of socks and shoes. The cuffs of his pants were rolled up to just below his knees. He looked more like a peasant boy, though a cigarette dangled from his lips. He drew a chair up so that he could face his mother, and lean into her closely.

"Mother, today has been a good day. I have convinced four boys to come with me," he told her as he reached for a cup of tea from the set beside her chair.

"Who? Who will go with you? I have fools and old men here," she responded.

"I went to the next village, and found two small boys and two young men. The boys are ages seven and eight and the young men ages fifteen and seventeen. The older ones are quite eager to leave their homes, but the younger ones I had to purchase to secure the deal."

"Then, your business is settled. You have what you came for," she stated hopefully.

"No, Ni-Ni! I need five young boys. I must return with five."

"You will have five days journey to reach your ship. In that journey, you can find many more young men, more than five, if you wish," she told him.

"Don't you want your young protégé to see the Gold Mountain? Don't you want him to grow rich like your sons?" he asked lightheartedly.

Threatened again, she spat her words at him, "He is mine. He is MY son! You cannot take what is not yours. I cannot let him go!"

"Mother," he said, as he sipped his tea reflectively. "*I am* your son. You have only five sons. I know how you gained this boy. You purchased him like you buy your pigs and oxen. That makes him property. Your five sons will inherit all that you own when you die. All that you have will become ours. So, you see Old Woman, everything you own is ours to have."

"Am I dead yet, that you take what you think you own?" She popped up swiftly from her chair to stand over him.

His eyes rose up to meet hers as he coolly sipped more tea. Without hesitation, he softly spoke in return, "Do you want to be?" he asked, his eyes never leaving hers.

In that one moment, it all became clear. Pao Chin was truly her son, flesh of her flesh, blood of her blood. He whispered death in her ear as though he could kill her easily, and just earlier in the day, she had plotted his death as a means of keeping her new son. She felt she could do it. She could kill him and cover up the nature of his visit. Her servants would keep quiet, and no one would question that Pao Chin had visited and left again as swiftly as he came. She would tell everyone that he got what he wanted and returned to his brothers and father in America. It would take months before her other sons would figure out Pao Chin was not coming back. It might also frighten the other sons from returning with any more threats to her property. She had pictured in her mind her youngest son rotting in a lonesome grave far removed from this house. She felt her skin crawl as she sat down hard into her chair again.

Both sat silently, as the battle waged in their minds. Pao Chin finished his tea and sat the cup back on its tray. He leaned closer to his mother. "Madam, your sons work hard so that we may make our fortunes. We hope to make you more gold. I must have one boy for each brother to ease their lives and help their businesses prosper. Your new son will have great opportunities there. He can even go to a western school and receive a proper education. I bet you have him attending that same worthless School of Confucius that you sent us to. I tell you, it is not the same in America. It is a place of big dreams and big places. He will grow to be a big man in a big country. Money still lines the streets there. This will be for the best." He lectured.

"He is the son I need for my old age. He will take over this land when I am too old or gone. I need him here," her voice was pleading. "I know that none of you, none of my five sons, will ever return to care for an old woman, or this land. The Gold Mountain has burned out your eyes and your hearts, never to return to the land that bore you. Would you rob me of my heart also?"

"Why don't you ask him," came his reply. His eyes motioned her to a distant doorway, where my father stood in the dark, listening.

"Child, you should not be here," she admonished.

"No! Come here boy and tell your Ni-Ni how you feel. I am your uncle. Come. Do you want to go with me to the Gold Mountain?" Pao Chin motioned for the boy to join them.

My father stepped forward. In his hand was a small ox carved from soft wood. It was his favorite toy that reminded him of Tak-Tak, the ox he rode to school. An elderly man had carved it for him when he was yet a baby.

"Ni-Ni: I could go to the Gold Mountain and make a fortune for both of us. I could send you much wealth. Maybe you could come with us? I heard the Gold Mountain is glorious." He said quickly directly to her.

"Oh! The dreams of glory and gold and riches. My sons are greedy…" she said softly.

Silence interrupted for a moment. "Already his head is filled with dreams. These dreams I cannot fulfill for him. He will leave me for them, won't he?" she stated, her heart sinking.

"Pao Chin," she finally asked, "how can we make our peace this day?"

"Give me what I want, and I will go. If you like, I promise never to return," he told her.

A pause grew as her mind made up her response. "Take the boy, but on one condition."

"Yes, Mother?" he sat forward to listen.

"Send me more gold and I will send you more servants to work for you, and all my sons, as I am able, and when you have enough, return this boy to me. Will you take an oath to this?" she proffered.

Pao Chin poured himself another cup of lukewarm tea. "This may take some time, Mother…but yes! I agree. I promise to return the boy, if you promise to send more workers for us as we need them."

My Father's eyes lit up, and they danced as he grinned at both of them. He was about to have his first real adventure, all the way to the Gold Mountain itself! Ni-Ni's fingers fluttered over his face, her eyes sad in retrospect. How long would it take for him to return, she asked herself?

It was hard for my father to sleep that night, he was so excited. But as sleep overtook him in the small hours of the morning, he dreamed of an old dragon that carried him below its massive wings. The dragon was old, losing its scales, and its once vibrant colors growing pale, its wings full of rips and tears. High over an unfamiliar landscape they soared, the dragon circled slowly, and as it banked and turned, he let loose his grip on my father, and he fell screaming into a new and foreign land.

Chapter 8

It was now 1926, and my father was six years old. He was about to leave this country he had always known. He could not remember his real parents. He had some vague memories of two older twin sisters, and the kindly but stern grandmother had bid him a tearful "goodbye" with many promises of his return whispered in her ear. She shrieked and fell into the arms of her servant girl as he ran down the house steps to join Pao Chin. The entire village had stopped their daily routines to gather round the strange conveyance that came to carry the prodigal son and "The One" away. It was a very beat-up, mechanical black truck that came miles and miles from the nearest city to pick them up. The owner was given a great deal of money to drive them back to Canton, and the ship that awaited them in its harbor.

Pao Chin had arranged for a girl and her mother to come to America in six months' time. He had purchased his bride, handling the seventeen-year-old virgin with softness and lust in his heart. She was a pure thing who stared at her shoes as he circled her, brushing the ends of her straight black hair with his fingertips. He imagined her pleading and squirming body on their wedding night. She was pretty enough, even for a country girl, to make his brothers envious. Perhaps the girl's mother would be interested in an American marriage to one of his brothers, but his mind did not linger on that thought. He arranged for their travel papers and gave money for their passage with instructions to follow him. Their immigration would be met at Angel Island where fake marriage papers would be produced to affect their release. This girl ignited his loins, and when he finished his business procuring her, he quickly went to visit his father's whore. She was older of course but welcomed him so that she could learn of news about his father and asked if she was being sent for. After satisfying himself, he tossed money at her and told her with a slight laugh that she would not be sent for now, or in the foreseeable future.

My Father had said his "goodbyes" earlier, and now his shiny eyes were cast upon a real motorized vehicle, with a stinky engine that belched and farted foul smells. The long flatbed part held sacks of vegetables, a squealing piglet and one goat tied to the side bars. Someone took his case of belongings and threw it in the back, along with his uncle's case. Then, two young boys and two older boys jumped into the flatbed and sat down among all the cases, food sacks and jugs of tea and water.

The journey was long and hard for a six-year-old, but the driver sang funny songs and was rewarded with American cigarettes. He also cooked their meals on the side of the roads they traveled, using the supplies taken from their village. The driver slept in the cab of the truck, while the uncle and my father slept on the flat bed. The other four boys slept on the ground. The company was amiable, but the four boys did not talk much in the company of his uncle. They made their own campfire and their own beds on the ground, well away from the man they knew as "Master Pao."

At night, my father fell asleep asking questions about the Gold Mountain, and what he would be doing there. The Uncle was kind enough, though he wearied of all the questions the closer they got to Canton. He asked the boy to call him Uncle Jimmy. Each brother had adopted an American name to better fit in with their new world, because most people could not pronounce their Chinese names. Christian names were also required of them by Immigration Officers who could not distinguish one Chinese name from another without given American names. So it was, that each brother took on a new name. Pao Chin was now "Jimmy" and his four brothers were "Andy"," "Sam" "Frank" and "Joey". But "Andy" did not like his new paper name much, and because of his small stature, those who knew him simply called him "Shorty". It never made sense to him, but he preferred the name of "Shorty" to "Andy".

Jimmy lived in Santa Barbara and owned a restaurant, a Chinese laundry and shoe repair store. Sam, the oldest, was in Chicago and had a Chinese-American restaurant which had a large bar. Frank lived in Sacramento California and owned a small café and a laundry house in a very small town. Joey lived in New York and worked as a dishwasher and sous chef in a prestigious steakhouse. Shorty lived in Los Angeles and was a bartender and a short-order cook in a Los Angeles restaurant called The Golden Buddha in old Chinatown. These were the typical jobs allowed under the laws of the land they occupied as immigrants.

My Father absorbed these stories like a thirsty sponge. He was thrilled. What new American name would he be given? He thought of a new school, tall buildings, education, riches, work and wealth. He day-dreamed of one day going back to his village to carry his old Ni-Ni to the new world. His youthful mind conjured up huge dreams. He would build her a new house, a palace made of solid gold and she would have many servants to wait on her.

His Uncle was kind enough and spoke gently to him, but every once-in-a-while, he would catch a glimpse of his uncle standing away from him, a cold, stony look on his face as he gazed hard at my father. It was a curious and almost threatening gaze that wasn't made clear until the day he stepped foot on board the ship that would carry him away from all he knew. That day finally came.

As my father stepped aboard the ship, they parted company with the four boys who traveled with them, and my father followed his uncle to a small stateroom. Inside, he found two beds, one table between the beds, and a round window on the far wall. It also held a small round mirror over a desk that held the first electrical lamp my father ever saw. It was tiny and cramped. As his uncle removed his hat and coat, he suddenly stopped what he was doing, grabbed my father's small arm and roughly escorted him outside the cabin, and abruptly slammed the door. Confused, my father pounded on the door to be let back in.

"Uncle, let me in!" he pleaded. The door flew open, and the ugly, stony look was back on his uncle's face. "You do not sleep here with me. Go to the others. Sleep with them. Sleep with the pigs. I do not care. But stay away from me until we reach our destination." With that said, Uncle Jimmy slammed the door, and to make certain, locked it.

Confused and frightened, my father stood for a moment, trying to work out what he should do. He ran back to the ship's deck to look for his cousins. He found the four boys squatting around in a circle at the back end of the ship. They were eating rice and vegetables given to them by an older man who carried the food in a large clay pot. Many Chinese were at this end of the ship. This deck at the stern of the ship was open to poorer passengers who gathered, much as many villagers would, to socialize and eat together. Their quarters far below deck were nothing more than dozens of hammocks in a tight and darkly lit space near where the engines were heard to grind and pump all day and night. So, these passengers stayed on this deck, often choosing to sleep up top, rather than risk the dank smells, stifling heat and noise of their sleeping quarters below.

When the four young boys were found to be traveling alone to the new world, an older man stepped forward and told them he would care for them, if they would offer him traveling companionship across the sea. He was also alone, and wanted their company so that his meals and his days would not be so lonely. This was his fourth trip to the Gold Mountain. He once worked on the transcontinental railroad and now lived in a place called Sacramento. It would be wonderful to pass the time telling these youth all about his adventures in the Gold Mountain.

The old man was pouring out tea from a jug for all four boys, when my father came up to them.

"May I join you brothers?" he asked. Not wanting to insult "The One", the boys quickly shifted their squatting circle to allow him room. "Young Master," queried the old man, "we saw you trail your uncle. Why do you not stay with him? Are you bored of his company already?"

With tears in my father's eyes, he explained to the others that perhaps he had insulted his uncle somehow because he was kicked out and told to join his cousins.

It was the seventeen-year-old boy who spoke in response. "You did nothing wrong. Your Uncle hates you and can tell you now."

"What do you mean?" my father asked.

"Before I left my home, I heard my parents speak of his anger with you. Your Uncle told my father that you are not an heir…of anything. All that belongs to the Dowager belongs to him and his brothers he said. He is not even your real uncle. Nor is he your brother. You are a servant to the Yee Family. A peasant like us, he said. You will work hard for these five brothers, and they will make sure you never go home again." The older boy grinned sardonically.

My father sat in silence; his arms wrapped around his knees. The old man proffered some tea, but he shook his head in decline, and as he did so, the tears escaped his eyes and fell upon his cheeks. He finally spoke, his voice quivering. "May I stay with you? I have no place to go." They answered him by drawing their crouched circle more closely to each other, drawing him in as they shifted.

My father understood the ruse and pretense. His uncle was kind until they were aboard this ship, and he could not escape to run away or return home. Feeling the waves beneath their boat, and watching the shoreline disappear in the far distance, my father knew he had no other place to go except where this ship would take them.

He wondered what would really happen to him now that he understood his dreams were to become the stuff of nightmares.

Chapter 9
Meet My Mother

It was 1938, and my mother was sixteen years old. She had blond hair made curly by bobby pins and pin curls. Her blue eyes danced below reddish-blond lashes. Her smile revealed large white teeth. She was considered in her Southern California community of Pasadena to be a pretty girl. And she knew it. In a sense, it made her feel powerful, and being the oldest of three children, she often took advantage of her high state of mind to rule the other two siblings by any means possible. She was very good at manipulation.

She was her daddy's little girl, and though she feared her stern mother, she knew her father would always cushion the near blows of her mother. Whenever her mother began to yell at her, or try to discipline her, her father always stepped in to deflect the seriousness of the mood, or to take the brunt of her mother's anger. Like a spoiled daughter, my mother felt invincible and impervious to the tortures and demands of a less than understanding mother.

Her father was a veteran of World War I and had suffered from back trouble sufficient to keep him from working full time jobs. He took odd jobs at will, working with his hands when there was work, and tinkering around home, or around neighbors' homes when there was no work to be had. It was her mother that was clearly the provider, and she never missed an opportunity to remind her husband, in front of their three children, that it was her money, and her job, that provided food on their table and paid the bills. But father and daughter remained thick as thieves, always in league against their badgering mother and wife.

My mother seemed to always get out of doing her chores and always had excuses for not doing as she was asked. She paid her younger siblings to do her portion of the housework. She would sweet-talk her father into running the expected errands her mother asked of her. She did not excel in school, scoring below average grades, because the work of being pretty and popular was ever more important.

This streak of rebellion that directed my mother's course of action was beginning to take its toll on my grandmother. It was then she made up her mind.

A Family counsel was called on one Sunday afternoon after dinner. There was an all-too-familiar seriousness to her mother's tone, and Laura Mae sat down in a zone of safety at her father's feet as he sat in his chair. Her brother and sister plopped on the sofa. My grandfather ran his hand over my mother's hair as he puffed on his pipe. The comforting smell of cherry tobacco instantly filled the room with its aromatics.

"Bonnie and Glenn, I want you to say goodbye to your sister Laura Mae," her mother began. Instantly the atmosphere in the room was charged with electricity, and all backs stiffened in response. "What?" "Papa, what did she say?"

"Laura Mae, you are leaving tomorrow to go live with your grandparents in Oregon," Laura Mae's mother said, her arms folded in front of her. Her stance appeared immovable.

Mother stood up quickly as if in defense of her life. She was ready to do battle. But before she could speak, her mother said, "Now, I don't want to hear another word about this, my mind is made up! You won't listen to me, your own mother, and you rebel against everything…" Her mother's voice began to rise.

"You can't do this! I won't go! You can't make me! You can't! Daddy, tell her I won't go…" A look of panic covered her pretty face as she turned to her father.

"Now, Princess, your mother and I feel this will be for the best." Her father replied reaching up for her arm.

Betrayal and abandonment hit her square in the gut. Her father had gone to the dark side. She was quick to pull away from his seeking hand. The look on her face told him everything, and he withdrew his hand, and puffed harder on his pipe, the top of the bowl glowing red hot.

My mother ran to her room, slamming the door as hard as she could. Her mother yelled at her all the way up the staircase, "It's all settled, Laura Mae. We're driving to the train station tomorrow morning. Deal with it, young lady. This is for your own good."

Father left the living room and opened the China cupboard in the dining room. He was pouring whiskey when the other two children ran up to him. "Pop, why's Laura Mae going to live with Granma and Granpa? Is she pregnant?"

The father reached out to slap his shoulder. Her sister chimed in. "Yeah, Pop, is she in big trouble, did she do something really bad this time?"

"Laura Mae doesn't do as she's told. You know she doesn't mind your mother one lick. Well, your mom's pretty tired of her rebelliousness, and you both know Laura Mae refuses to listen to me, her mother and anyone else. We both agree that if she doesn't get straightened out soon, she could be a worse place than this. And no! She isn't pregnant or in big trouble! She is willful and stubborn. Where do you kids get them ideas? Laura Mae just doesn't listen to her mother is all. Living with Grandpa Willy and

Granny Mel will do her a world of good. Living on a farm, working hard, why she'll come home gentle as a lamb in no time," he told them, unconvinced. "And if the two of you don't toe the line, we can send you far away, too!" The two siblings scattered madly for their rooms.

After a fitful and sleepless night, Laura Mae Storms found herself standing apart from her own Family, eyes red, puffy and swollen, head down in shame, waiting for the one o'clock train to Eugene, Oregon. Wanting to run but failing to think of a single place she could find safe harbor, my mother stared down at her suitcase and her own two shoes. It would take a great deal of time before she would forgive her Family for this betrayal. She felt she could never forgive her mother. Ever. Her young brother and even younger sister wanted to share her sadness and fear, but found themselves too amused with her leaving, too enthralled at the wonder and beauty of Los Angeles' Union Station, and too excited to see the train coming to share in her self-pitying moment.

As the train pulled into the station, jets of steam were released, filling the platform with dramatic clouds that enhanced the equally dramatic moment.

"Now, you be sure to wait for your grandparents at the other end, ya hear?" yelled her mother over the noise of the engines. Her father quickly gave her a bag filled with fashion magazines and candy bars. "Here, I bought you some things for your trip. I love you, Honey. I know you'll have a great time." He reached out to hug her and my mother stood quite still and as responsive as a stone statue. He hesitated in letting her go, and decided to whisper in her ear as the hug lingered. "Don't worry, Princess. I'll work on your mom, and you'll be able to come back before the summer's out." Words and promises made too late.

"Laura Mae, give me a hug, too," her mother said. This request spurred my mother to board the train with haste, not looking back. "Well, have it your way, Laura Mae, but I swear you'll miss me, like I'll miss you. I want you to write us. Let us know how you're doing. I'll certainly be writing and calling my parents for news, I can assure you. Don't you disappoint me, young lady, and don't do anything to embarrass me. They have my permission to whip you into shape literally!" Her mother's irritating voice grew faint as Laura Mae entered the train's compartment area, the sliding door closing behind her. After the porter helped her put her suitcase in the overhead compartment and took her ticket, she took her seat, her eyes never leaving her shoes.

Chapter 10

It was five o'clock in the morning, as my father bounded out of his bed. It was 1937, and at age seventeen, it was a struggle to wake so early in the morning, but he wanted this job badly enough to make the effort. It would take him fifteen minutes to wash, shave, and put on his uniform. He wore black silk house pants, soft slippers and a crisp, highly starched white linen Chinese jacket. My father was a "house boy" for the Santa Barbara "Home of Ramona" estate.

The ranch was known as the "Home of Ramona" because the Californio lifestyle was the actual setting for the novelist Helen Hunt Jackson's romantic and fictional 1884 novel *Ramona*.

Just east of Piru, California, the ranch was the original home of Californio Ygnacio del Valle, a onetime original alcalde of Los Angeles and member of the California State Assembly. The setting of this ranch, once visited by Jackson, was brilliantly and romantically described in her novel, so much so, that tourists and fans of the book came from cities and countries all over the world to visit.

In 1937, the ranch was sold by the del Valle family and now belonged to Mary and August Rubel, who were painstakingly restoring the ranch to its former glory days.

Here, my father was given room and board and qualified to be a house servant during a time when Asian houseboys were very chic among the nouveau riche.

The Charlie Chan films popularized the stereotypical

Chinese American. His job was to keep the main house clean, bring in the mail, bring in the newspapers and serve his Patrons with tea and sandwiches at various times, serve meals whenever guests arrived, or a formal dinner was planned, and he made sure fresh flowers were placed in all the useable rooms. It made his mistress happy if he bowed low and moved quickly through his duties without appearing underfoot. She dressed him in a black silk pajama set with soft black slippers during the day, and a crisp white linen suit for formal occasions. People smiled at him, but no one ever spoke to him except to instruct or require something of him. It suited the owners to have a fashionable houseboy, so very popular at the time among rich white people.

He understood what it meant to work for White people. His uncle and grandfather taught him that all Caucasians were "Gwailo" or "White Devils" or even more derogatory, "White Ghosts". He was taught to smile and "kowtow" in their presence and to spit and deny their existence when they were not looking. He was encouraged to hate, but that feeling of disparity and prejudice did not come easily to my father, despite their early attempts to warn him and teach him as a child to share their bigotry. The silk pajama look pleased his employers, but he failed to find it a stereotypical offense. He liked everything about this new Country.

At seventeen years, Father's grasp of the English language was crude, in its origins, but he watched and listened, and was determined to eradicate his accent. He loved going to the cinema and watching American film, repeatedly, memorizing dialogue and mouthing along to the screen nearly all of the spoken words. Because the cucina, or kitchen, was removed from the main house of Ramona, he sang along to the radio he was allowed to play in the kitchen. The radio, music, songs, movies all taught him English.

As a teen, my father wanted and needed to belong to this new society of wealthy White people. He wanted to imitate their habits, their speech, their clothing. With every spare dollar, he bought clothing that matched what was being worn. He joined the Santa Barbara Tennis Club and became a fair contender. Though he could not afford a car alone, he did go in with three other Chinese friends and purchased a 1937 Plymouth sedan. In the company of his Asian friends, he insisted they all speak English, and though most were dating Asian girls in the area, my father enjoyed the company of American girls, though those dates were hard to find. But in groups of youth, standing next to a young White girl was hardly a date. He very much liked being here in California. He stopped dreaming of old Ni-Ni, his village, and no longer had thoughts of returning to China. These thoughts pretty much ended after his Uncle Jimmy pulled him out of school at the age of 9 to work in his laundry house. The cruelty of his uncle never ended but seemed to exponentially increase with each year and with each job.

He often reflected on how he had entered this country. Though his uncle had papers to re-enter the United States through Angel Island's Immigration station, my father, and the other four boys did not. Each were confined to the Island's male barracks, segregated from the women and girls and made to go through a series of questioning by the Immigration officers.

Though he was then seven years old, my father and most of the other young boys, did not understand the questioning, and each had failed to satisfy their captors. Fortunately, the older men passed along answers to them, and quietly, over meals, or doing laundry, or bathing in the open-air courtyard, the old men tutored the young boys into a recitation and memorization of the answers that would win their freedom. These little papers were passed along, found under plates, in pockets, mysteriously stuffed in their hands when they awoke. Once, father witnessed a man stuff such a note in his mouth, chewed and swallowed it. It was safe to assume that if these notes were found, they would be in dire trouble with their captors.

"Your village has five pigs, two horses, and thirteen houses," they whispered when the guards were not looking. "Say it!" They required all to repeat the answers. They told him the name of a village, though it was not the village he came from. They told him the name of his Family, though it was not true. It made little sense to him, because his village had more than five pigs and twenty-three houses, but he dutifully repeated and memorized until the day his interview came.

With the help of a Chinese interpreter, an Immigration Officer, asked my Father to sit in the chair before his desk. The room was dark, except for a lamp on the desk. The Officer made my father nervous. The officer had such pale skin and red curly hair. He sat on his hands to keep them still, as he waited. He answered all the preliminary questions, gave them answers as he understood them, and then he was asked, "How many pigs and horses and houses do your village have?" Father hesitated, and then he recited slowly, "My village has five pigs, two horses and thirteen houses," he replied swallowing hard. There was talk in a language he did not understand, papers were stamped and written upon. They talked of assigning an American name because his name was too difficult to spell or pronounce. They asked the boy, and he said nothing, looking confused. Finally, referring to a list on his desk, the Immigration Officer wrote on his records the new name of this boy who was about to be released onto American soil. He wrote, *David Lee Fong*.

While he had always enjoyed the view of San Francisco Bay from atop the walls of his confinement, nothing could match the short ferry ride to the San Francisco docks. He smiled all the way, happy to be in the company of his friends, the two youngest boys he had traveled with from China. Their new American-Chinese names were *Henry Lee Fong* (having been interviewed just after my father) and *Daniel Joseph Chou*. All three boys were happy to be set free and on their way to new adventures. The older two boys were released earlier, and it was supposed they would meet up and join them wherever they were. It was terribly disappointing when their "Uncle" Jimmy was waiting for them at the terminal.

Standing sternly, smoking a cigarette, Uncle Jimmy flicked the fag into the water as the three boys came down the boat ramp. Their smiles faded, and they looked down at their shoes. Without speaking, Uncle motioned to the doorway, and all three followed the direction of his finger.

Though they did not speak, or smile, each boy communicated with small touches, staying tightly together, their heads and eyes turning in every direction. What a strange place this was. The building was massive, with a long string of cloudy windows at the top of high metal and wooden walls. They had never seen a building stand so high or one so very long. The end of the building appeared not to have doors, but stood so wide, all they could see was blue sky beyond its edges. Then, they stood where many, many cars sat one behind the other. Jimmy had stepped forward and opened one to the back seat. They piled into the back seat of this wondrous and warm car, and were delighted with all of the surroundings, the noise, the whistles of distant boats, and the smells never before encountered. Their little heads crammed up against the windows to better see out as Uncle got behind the wheel and drove away. The water, boats and piers faded away to scenes of massive buildings, and then houses all built on hills with materials unfamiliar to them. The streets were lined with trees and there were not enough green plants; the colors were different, and no animals could be found on the streets. People seemed overdressed, everyone wore hats, and automobiles were everywhere. Father saw a woman whose dog was tethered to her arm as they walked. The dog was harnessed liked an ox on a rope. The dog seemed to be pulling her down the street.

The stories of the Gold Mountain told of streets being lined with precious stones, silver and gold. It must have been that each boy looked carefully wherever the car turned, so as not to miss their chance to view the open treasure. So far, the grey and black material the car drove on did not appear to be like gold.

They rode for about fifteen minutes in silence, the three young boys glued to their windows. At last, the car entered familiar territory, and the smells and sights changed dramatically. Father, and the others, spotted Chinese symbols, vegetables and fruits in boxes outside shops, and people who were dressed differently, but undoubtedly were their countrymen.

As if night turned to another day, father and his companions exited the car and viewed as well as smelled what appeared to be a city in China. Of course, they were in San Francisco's Chinatown district, but fresh off the boat, they had no idea where they were. It was as though they had traveled to another distant shore and found life just as they had left it back in the City of Canton. It felt as though their world extended days and months beyond their own shores. Except this city was more modern, held taller buildings, and had all the appearances of being brighter and perhaps cleaner than those in China. The weather was cooler, too.

Uncle Jimmy pointed to the inside of the door he was holding open, and all three boys stepped into a restaurant. At last Uncle Jimmy spoke and ordered them to go all the way to the back room. Marching past the counter space and booths where happy compatriots were consuming bowls of noodles and what smelled like roasted pig, my father became aware of his own hunger. He and the boys had not eaten for many hours.

Coming into a larger room, filled with empty tables, the boys found several men at a large round table near the back wall. They were drinking tea. Plates of delicious looking food filled the middle of their round table, and chopsticks flew between plates and bowls of rice held up to their mouths. My Father's own mouth was watering now.

Uncle Jimmy herded the boys in front of him and spoke in Chinese to the oldest man who sat with a piece of cloth tucked into his shirt collar. As the old man listened, he sipped his tea, and set the cup down. He replied "good, good" in his native tongue, and motioned for Jimmy to set the boys up at the next table.

Immediately, women brought out bowls of steaming rice, an entire roasted chicken cut in pieces, and a noodle soup with greens. Setting chopsticks, cups and teapots in front of the boys, they dived into the food as though it were their last meal. Jimmy joined the men at their table, and while my father tried to listen to their hushed conversation, he was too eager to eat, and fell into his food instead of eavesdropping.

What he failed to grasp until later was who the old man was.

After bellies were filled, and cigarettes were lit, the old man removed the napkin from the top of his shirt and set it down on his plate, motioning to my father to come to him. Little David did not hesitate and dutifully approached the old man.

"So, this is the little Prince, is it?" he said aloud. Jimmy's smile was sardonic, and the others smiled, but with sneers. Father looked around the room at these men and gathered from their expressions they did not like him.

"You remember your parents, boy?" The old man asked.

"No," came his reply.

"Do you know that they sold you?" he questioned further.

"Yes."

"You know that boy babies can fetch a fine sum, if sold? How then does a child who is sold for very much money gain such favor with an old woman? After all, you were a costly purchase as a slave."

"A slave? I did not know," remarked the boy.

"Why do you think you are here now, boy?"

"I – I will work and earn great wealth for my uncle, and he will send gold to Ni-Ni and she will come live here in the Gold Mountain, and…"

The room erupted with laughter, and it made my father smile, too.

"That old woman will never leave China, boy. Never!" the old man said.

"Then, I will carry gold back with me, and I will take it home to her," he replied, his words sounding uncertain and softly spoken.

More laughter brought more chatter from the men and my father's eyes fell to the floor knowing his answers were not well received by the others.

The old man grabbed his small shoulders with both hands and drew him closer. The gesture made my father look up into the old man's face.

"Boy, do you know who I am?" he asked as he looked into

the boy's eyes.

My Father shook his head wordlessly.

"I am your grandfather, boy. The old woman in China is my wife. These are my five strong sons. We left China a long time ago to come to the Gold Mountain. Your Uncle Jimmy was sent back to China to (and here he hesitated just slightly) *rescue* you from the old woman and bring you here. Do you understand?" He pressed on, not waiting for a response.

"You and your cousins were brought here so that you can work for us and make us great fortunes. You will be richer here than in your homeland. We all work together to make great money. With great wealth comes great power, grandson. Do you understand now?" He said looking at the boy.

"Work is good," came a meager reply. "Are you really my grandfather, Sir?"

"Eh? No. You were sold to me. That means I own you, but no! Because of those black bastards, this country has a problem with slavery and owning other humans. So, no! You must be my grandson so that the authorities believe you are in our Family. And you are in our Family because we own you, so, yes! I am your grandfather, and these men are your uncles!" He laughed at his logic.

The uncles laughed in agreement.

The boy was confused.

"Shall I call you, 'grandfather' then," he pressed.

"Yes, yes, of course, as good as anything," the man replied. "I am your 'Grandpa Harry'!"

"What work will you have me do, Sir?" The boy asked weakly.

"Ho! A wise and eager young boy! This day, you will go with your Uncle Jimmy, and you must do all he asks you to do. You must never question him. You must always obey. In return, he will feed you well, buy you clothes, and you can enjoy life as a young boy in this great country. Is that not a good thing?" said his grandfather.

"And what of Henry and Daniel? Will they come, too?" My father asked, glancing at Henry and the other boy, who were listening intently.

"No, no," came his reply. "One will go with Uncle Shorty to Los Angeles, and the other will go with Uncle Frank to the beautiful city Sacramento.

"Where are the two older boys?" he asked, emboldened.

"They are going back with Sam and Joey to work with them far away in the east," came the reply. "Now, go, sit with the other boys while we talk."

Father turned and walked just as dutifully back to his table. As he sat down, a woman came to clear the plates, and wipe the table off. She put a plate of almond cookies down in front of the boys, as she gathered cups and plates. With the woman shielding the children from the men, Henry immediately broke down in tears and whispered to the other two.

"I don't want to go! He sobbed. "I don't want to be split up! What will become of us?"

"Sh-h-h! You must not cry, not now. My Uncle will beat us both!" my father cautioned him.

Henry put his face into his arms, and tried to silence both his tears and his fear. Daniel looked flushed in his face as though he might also cry, and my father felt his own fear communicate with the other two.

"We were purchased, bought for a sum of coin, and brought here to be slaves. They own us. We are like the Coolies. Just as others worked for Old Ni-Ni, we now are workers to these men. We must go and do as they say. We have no way back home. We have no other choice. We must be brave. If we work hard, if we are strong, perhaps we can run away and find each other," my father's voice grew hopeful.

"Yes," Daniel said, his voice wavering, "we can find each other again. We can run away."

"How shall we find each other?" Henry asked, "We don't even know where we are."

Henry's point deflated the two others immediately. How would they find each other. The names of Los Angeles, and Sacramento sounded very foreign, very far away and difficult to remember. None of the boys had even seen a map of the world, much less held a vision of where they were now in relation to where they were yesterday.

"Our uncles know where we are going and where the others are. Our uncles send packages to my Ni-Ni; perhaps we can send letters or packages to each other," my father said. "If we do all that we are asked, if they are pleased with us, we can ask to send letters, or packages to one another. Maybe even ask to visit each other!" He was excited at the thought, and the other two boys felt more hopeful, and their eyes lit up at the thought of being back together one day.

It gave them hope. These three, more than the older two, played and talked and slept with each other for the forty days it took to reach land. They ran on the deck of their ship like free spirits in control of all that they surveyed while at sea. The old man that took care of them fed them and gave them a warm place to sleep. Their tummies were filled each day with good food. They stayed together for the entire voyage. Sometimes the ship's officers and crew would let them follow them as though they were in charge of something. Their world became a microcosm of life on board ship, and it was filled with the kind of joy that comes with being little boys. They had no worries until they reached land. And now this threat to tear them from each other was almost too much to bear.

"" We must remember which uncle has who," my father said firmly.

"How? He did not say which of us would go with which uncle," countered Daniel.

Henry said, "But you go with Uncle Jimmy…we all know who he is." All three glared across the table directly at the venomous uncle.

"Then you both must vow to find me," declared my young Father. He grabbed the hand of both boys and instructed them. "You both must be good sons, good boys. If your uncles like you, and have no cause to beat you, you will find out where Uncle Jimmy lives, and then you will find me. Send me letters. Tell me where you are. What you are doing. Find me and I will find you both."

"We will find each other," Daniel smiled.

Though Henry remained scared and a bit skeptical, he forced a small smile, and squeezed the hand of the other two boys. "Then, we will run away, and be together again," Henry whispered.

During the time he was a little boy, yet new to this country, he knew his uncle and his grandfather would not support his wants and desires. He understood that he was chattel to them. This revelation came to him quite clearly the day he was pulled from his American school at the age of 9 to work in his 'uncle's laundry house. He was required to stand on a wooden crate and feed sheets, shirts and pants into an ironing press for ten hours a day.

On one occasion, a White man wearing a badge entered the laundry house where Father was stationed by the front window. When his uncle came out to greet the Officer, he informed Uncle he was a Truant Officer, and asked why the boy in the front window was not in school. From then on, the front shade was drawn, and Father worked under a lamp for illumination. But that did not work very long, and the Truant Officer returned with the help of a local police officer. "The boy must be allowed to go to school. That is the law in this Country," they shouted at Father's Uncle. Loud words in Chinese and English were exchanged. Confrontations with American law enforcement always forced Uncle to retreat to his native tongue, as he spoke in his worst broken English that he did not understand, even though he plainly did. From then on, Father and his iron press and his lamp were removed to the basement, behind a locked door, where discovery was nearly impossible. Here, he toiled, pressing, folding, burning his small fingers and listening to western radio, Jack Benny and Red Skelton variety shows, in the dimly lit basement where he slept and ate. Fresh air was a treat, and trips to his 'uncle's restaurant on weekends gave him greater views of his western world, and he hoped and dreamt for a better day. He often thought of Henry and Daniel and believed they were doing the same things he was; only miles away in other towns he could not imagine where.

The 'better day' came in his sixteenth year when given twenty dollars, he was asked to go to the market for fresh crabs for a special dinner. It was a new spring day. The air was fresh in Los Angeles, cleared and made sweet by a soft and gentle breeze that caressed his hair and lifted his shirt collar. It put a bounce to his step. He walked toward the fish market, but on his way, found several people waiting for a bus. There he found in the small crowd a young Chinese man he knew to have worked for a while at his 'uncle's restaurant. He called out to him.

"Hey, Tim! Where you headed?" He asked.

"David, right? I'm going to a new job in Santa Barbara," came Tim's reply.

"Where is that exactly?" My Father asked. He did not know his boundaries, how large Los Angeles was, nor what lay beyond the undefined borders of his world.

"It's just up the coast, nice town," Tim answered.

"How much does a bus to Santa Barbara cost?" my father ventured.

"It's two dollars one way, why?" Tim asked.

Fingering the twenty-dollar bill in his pocket, Father weighed his options. It seemed so simple. He wondered why he didn't think of doing this earlier. He was in America. Hell! He *was* an American! This was the Land of the free and home of the brave. He could do what he was told and buy crabs, or he could take the next bus to who- knows- where and be free at last! "Do you think I can come with you?" David asked.

With no luggage and no regrets, Father joined up with Timothy Lee for a whole new adventure north of Los Angeles where his uncle and grandfather would not find him and didn't even know where to begin to search and where he experienced his first real taste of American freedom.

Chapter 11

Uncle Jimmy, or Pao Chin Yee, was a suspicious man. He trusted no one, except perhaps his Father Harry. He shared the same contempt for the White masters of this world that his own father did. From this contempt, he embraced a meanness that comes from a heart turned to stone. He wore it like a well-earned badge upon a cynical face. He was better than his Caucasian counterparts. He rose above them. They tried to beat him down. They tried to keep him in his place, but he knew in his heart they were white trash. After all, his civilization, his roots, his history was longer, richer and more successful than anyone else he knew. He was superior.

Jimmy felt like a rich man in a country that wanted to suppress him. He now owned a restaurant In Oakland, California, he called The Right Way Cafe, and two Chinese laundry shops. He employed both Chinese and Caucasian employees. He made their lives equally miserable as a boss. It made him feel powerful. It made him feel like a king, and he was taught from the master of superiority, his own father, Harry Yee.

Power, he learned, came in the form of money. Money could buy anything. A beggar in the street could rise up to be a powerful and respected man if clothed in the garment's money could buy. Money solved all problems. You could own the local police, just as his own father did, if you paid them well enough. Money brought you respect. No one talked down to him, nor talked back when he held their payroll. Money was what built his little empire of business and good fortune, and money is what got him out of bed each morning, hungry for more.

Jimmy rarely thought of his old life in China. He was the youngest of five sons. His father and mother owned a great deal of land in China, and had many who worked for them. As a boy growing up in China he had naught to do but play and explore, fish, and play tricks on the young servant girls while his four older brothers were in school. He had never seen any town or big city outside his village. He knew the surrounding villages, and they all knew who he was because his Parents were powerful people. He saw, at an early age, how others kowtowed to his parents.

It played a bit on his youthful mind that it was good to have such powerful Parents, and to know that land made you powerful, if the land was well-cared for and tended to. Since childhood, he understood the leisure of life, and the joy and freedom that wealth provided them.

He also understood that more was better. His parents fought about this all the time. His father enjoyed the comforts of his life. He had servants in his house, people who tended his fields, food enough for all, including trade to the nearest villages and towns. His purse was heavy with coin. His back, and the backs of his family, bore the weight of silk robes, heavy with embroidery and thick, warm layers. He had concubines housed in nearby villages, and life was delicious when he could steal away on the pretense of business. Yet, no matter how often his father was gone, the moment he returned, his mother would pursue the same argument in predictable fashion.

She wanted more. She demanded that he bargain for more land from each of the surrounding villages. She insisted that they drive off the encroaching villagers, take over their land, and incorporate themselves into larger wealth and greater land. The more land, she insisted, the greater their power and wealth.

Little Pao Chin observed these arguments in silence. He saw his mother's pleading eyes and grasping hands. He then saw his father's grimacing face, and threatening body language. He understood how his father hated these arguments, and how generally he ran off to avoid striking his mother for her strong tongue.

One day, he was called to the house, and when he entered dirty from his play, and smelling of sun and soil, he found his four brothers, and his mother and father sitting down. The servant girls poured tea and were asked to leave.

"I have a solution," his father spoke. "You wish more land and to expand our boundaries. I agree this will bring us greater power and greater resources. It may also gain the attention of rival warlords eager to assume our wealth." He looked at the weary face of his wife, already becoming an old crone, to make sure she was listening before he continued.

"We need more business, and our remoteness from China's wealthy cities is beyond our boundaries of operation. After all, we are peasant farmers, are we not?" He glanced at her again, before moving on. His wife sat with a stone face, but her eyes moved rapidly, shifting back and forth, as her mind engaged. Where was he going with this string of thought?

"No, we need new opportunity in order to improve our wealth. I propose that we travel to the Gold Mountain." He looked her in the eye, and waiting for a response. Her face shifted to dark brooding.

"I will not leave my home, Husband," she announced. "Land is wealth. What good is it if we give it up for sale. It only makes someone else wealthy. Besides, women are not yet permitted entry to the Gold Mountain."

"You misunderstood Wife," he retorted. "Our land will remain in our control, but to satisfy your desire for more land, we need more, much more income."

"Then," she said haltingly, "you propose to go to the Gold Mountain, and we stay here?"

"Again, you misunderstand, my wife," he repeated. "I cannot do this venture alone. I must, we must, have the help of each of our sons. They will go with me to the Gold Mountain and you will stay here to expand our interests."

His wife jumped from her sitting position, as though her seat caught fire beneath her. "You cannot suggest leaving me all alone while you travel to a new world beyond my reach. It is preposterous!"

"Is it so preposterous a suggestion that if I can earn more gold in one year there, that with five young and strong sons, I could earn five times more gold to send you each year we are gone?" He smiled slighting, knowing her greed would surface, and overtake her fears of abandonment.

The old woman stopped to calculate five times the weight of gold. She walked slowly around the chairs of her sons gathered in their Family circle. Four boys were indeed youthful and strong. Three were already more than eighteen years, and the other two, eager and young, could learn much more of trade and commerce than inside their little realm. Beyond that thought, was the core of her dreams, and that was of power. She wanted not just wealth, but the power over others that came with it. You could buy anything with money, and all other surrounding villages bowed to those who had the most wealth. Land meant wealth, and the more land she could gobble up under her control, the more power she could gain. The thoughts racing one after another, made her head swim, and she felt slightly dizzy from the affects. She hastened to her bench and sat down to catch her breath.

"How long do you propose to be gone?" she asked.

"It is impossible to say," he answered. "I must write letters to our cousins in San Francisco. I must secure their help in entering the country with all five sons. I'll need to gain travel papers. It will be costly just getting there. Once there, we will have to secure housing, jobs. I must assess what could make us the most wealth in the shortest time possible. You know our cousin is rich in the mercantile business. We may have to become merchants. Our sons may have to do hard labor while I work to set up a shop or two. Again, I remind you such wealth may take time, but will be more abundant with all of us working toward the same goal."

"Yes, yes. I see your point. Yes, we will all be working for the same goal," she said breathlessly. Alarms were going off in her head, and she could barely respond, her mind overwhelmingly engaged in a battle of "what-if's" versus "incalculable amounts."

It was the next day that Pao Chin learned the truth of his Father's plan. He had accompanied his father to the nearest village on the pretext of writing letters for travel papers. While he set about instructing the local teacher to draft letters to his cousin in San Francisco in America and letters with which to travel, he and Jimmy came to the familiar house of his favorite concubine.

As always, he was instructed by his father to wait outside, and was given food, drink and a playmate to keep him amused. The youth was younger than him, and he wasn't much interested. He waited for about ten minutes then rounded the corner of the house nearest the open windows of the sleeping area. Whenever he wanted to learn of his father's plans, or feelings, or complaints, he always used this position to eavesdrop on their bed conversation. He, of course, often heard their lovemaking, but as of late, his father seemed hasty, and it took a very short matter of minutes before he heard them talking. On this trip, he learned the truth of their journey to the Gold Mountain.

"Her greed is always of first importance, and with this journey, I will at last be free of her," his father softly stated.

"And what of this one who holds your heart? What shall I do without you to pleasure and comfort you?" asked his chattel. "I suppose I can easily be replaced."

"You I will send for," came his reply.

"I – I will go to the Gold Mountain, too?"

"It will take some time. Only certain wives can come into the country, but I can arrange to send for you to be my wife, or perhaps the wife of one of my sons," he told her.

She was giggling, and with her giggling, Pao Chin heard his father's soft laughter. "I will be rid of my nagging wife, I will have all my sons at my side, I will become a wealthy man and I will have you to give me comfort and pleasure." Pao Chin heard kissing and moaning again and turned away from his post under the window.

He had no intention of letting his mother know what he overheard. He never did. He learned a great deal and giving up this source of learning was unthinkable. He liked to spy. It would gain him nothing by telling all that he overheard. In fact, he was sure to be punished by either or both parents for such a deed. If he did, he felt he would forfeit his right to go to the Gold Mountain and that would be intolerable to stay behind alone without his father and his older brothers. So, he remained silent.

In the days and months that followed, young Pao Chin stayed

quiet but kept his eyes and ears opened. He witnessed the fights between his mother and father escalate in fury and frustration. His mother now threw things, stayed in her room and was sullen, her eyes downcast, as she roamed the hallways and rooms like an empty ghost. She no longer allowed her servants to bath her, dress her, or comb her hair. Her long hair, tinged with a few gray strands, was disheveled and greasy, and hid her beleaguered face. She did not appear to eat and refused all comfort and company. The screaming was inevitable whenever the two found themselves in the same room together. Soon, his father chose to stay away, and complete his travel arrangements in the house of his favorite concubine. This action left his sons home to endure constant wailing. The older ones left for the homes of their friends and their women, leaving poor Pao Chin alone and torn apart by the choices made by others.

  The day finally came, and his father and brothers descended upon the house, quickly gathering their clothing and the treasures of home they would take with them on their journey. They packed quietly, and without much excited talk. Their mother had fallen silent days ago within her rooms, and they did not wish to invite a final scene of desperation and guilt as they prepared to leave her.

  Within an hour, all five boys waited outside in the cool morning air for their father to emerge from the house. They would take horses and wagons to Canton where a ship awaited them, bound for San Francisco.

  Jimmy remembered the journey and its fascinating highlights. In the City of Canton, his father took them to a local tailor where each son was outfitted with a white linen western traveling suit. His older brothers were delighted with their new white Panama hats. Jimmy wore itchy wool pants that stopped and buckled at his knees. He was bothered by the stockings and shoes he had to wear. The top button of his shirt conspired to choke him before they would reach the Gold Mountain.

The ship was massive in his eyes, at least his memory of it. The sights and smells of the crew, the shiny wooden deck and railings were smooth to his touch. The stewards were clean in their white uniforms, but the crew that ran between closed doors appeared sweaty and smelled, their faces were scruffy with beards, and for the first time in his life, he saw men with white skin and round eyes. Some even had eyes the color of the blue sky, and this fascinated him. Though this was a freighter that took on passengers, Jimmy and his brothers were waited on by what they considered to be their servants during this voyage. The boy filled his days with hard play between decks, and made a nuisance of himself in the boiler and engine rooms below in the belly of the ship. He was always washed and cleaned at his morning meal with his family, but toward early evening, he came to the table worn, dirty, his clothing reduced to his undershirt, and undershorts.

Though for Jimmy the voyage seemed too short, Harry and his five sons finally arrived at the Port of San Francisco. They were met by a small contingent of "business" partners who had already cleared their entry into this country as incoming businessmen involved in the import of China's goods to America. Harry indeed, brought with him exports of jade, pottery, grains, spices and silks. He also brought letters and business papers for his partners. Upon brief inspection, their stories lined up, and their travel papers were found in order. Harry and his five sons stepped onto American soil, the beginning of their Gold Mountain journey.

Not being able to see much more than small hills in the

distance beyond the waters he journeyed over, young Pao Chin, now known in this new world as Jimmy, wondered which hill was considered to be the Gold Mountain?

Jimmy grew under the tutelage of his older brothers, and the community of Chinese they lived among. He did not have to attend school anymore and was taught to never leave the boundaries of their small Chinatown community. Jimmy rarely traveled with his father beyond the confines of San Francisco's Chinatown.

He worked at a restaurant washing dishes and peeling shrimps. He was never allowed in the main restaurant where the diners ate because of his age. No one wanted the authorities investigated their crew of child labor. From all this hiding and staying out of sight of white men, Jimmy learned that these authorities of another country could be tricked and lied to in order to maintain an image of compliance.

He witnessed his own father speak in broken English, feigning comprehension and obedience to laws, when questioned by those officials who came by to investigate the legitimacy of his father's businesses and business partners. But as soon as these authorities left, his father would spit, calling them filth under his breath, and the contempt was clear. The lessons were equally clear. If you could smile, bow, scrape and kowtow in front of these white devils, you could run your businesses pretty much anyway you wanted to, or needed to when the contemptible devils were gone.

So, Jimmy grew, and as he grew, he learned from everything he witnessed, and watched the exchange of money fall into the hands of his controlling father. His father took nearly all of the money made by his five sons, leaving them little more than living expenses that were meager and minimal.

Jimmy slept in a back room with two other Chinese, and all worked seven days a week, twelve to fourteen hours a day. His oldest brother would prepare a box for their mother which was mailed each Chinese New Year to their China home. He saw the gold that was hidden in the spice jars and knew that it was not half of what his father could have sent, but knew that for a while, this would satisfy his mother, and allow her to purchase more land.

One day, a young villager from a neighboring farm was brought in from China to work for one of his business partners. It was always important to hear news from those who entered the country. People had an easier time keeping up with what was going on in their homeland by those who bore news first-hand. The young teen told his new "uncle" of the Yee Village, and how their mother was prospering without her husband and sons.

It was this youth's story that brought the news of my small father who, they were told, was purchased from a poor family in order to become heir to the lands that did not belong to him. The news was disturbing to Harry, and he set about deciding for Jimmy to go home and assess the truth of the situation and deal with it. Harry had travel papers drawn up which allowed Jimmy to re-enter China and bring his new "bride" to America.

Harry was generous in telling Jimmy that he could return with a bride, if he found one to his liking. It was offered as a reward for spying on his own mother. He was instructed to find out what threat this male child was to his Chinese kingdom, and just what his wicked wife was up to. He was to find out if the village remained powerful among all the others and if its borders were expanding as he had hoped. He was skeptical about the sanity of his old wife after the many years of absence from her husband and sons. Jimmy was to ascertain if she was capable of running their village, or if it was suffering under her watch, and if someone needed to return for good.

    Jimmy, now twenty-five years old, was not thrilled at the prospect of such a long journey home, but he perked up at the idea of finding a wife. He used prostitutes to satisfy the urges of his manhood, but the idea of a wife would change how he was treated by his older brothers who had no wives and continued to sleep in communal living spaces. If he brought back a bride, he would gain their respect (he felt his brothers always treated him like a child) and he would be in a position to ask his father for a living wage and an apartment all their own. The self-importance of this pleased him greatly as he agreed to do his father's bidding and make the long trip home to China.

Chapter 12

Laura Mae was mucking out the two stalls that held her grand parents' milking cows. Wiping the sweat from her forehead, she breathed through her mouth in order to avoid the heavy smell of animal waste mixed with straw. Her list of expected chores was so long she rarely had time to contemplate how she got here in the first place. The busyness of her daily schedule anesthetized her from the feelings of wrath and abandonment. The microcosm of her new world locked out any feelings for the mother that placed her here, and the family that turned their backs on her. Here, she did not acknowledge feelings, but rather gave herself over to the compassion she felt for the elderly grandparents that simply needed her help in every way. The selfishness of her teen years gave way to a heart that grew large and increased in capacity, even in the wet, gray and dreary skies of Oregon.

The tiny town of Drain, Oregon was deep inside Douglas County, midway between the Oregon lumber mills of Coos Bay and the rich farmland of Roseburg, and just southwest of the growing city of Eugene, Oregon. It was a little blip of a town with a population of 289 people. The animals outnumbered their human populace.

Laura Mae had plenty of time to think. When she calmed down, when she lay in her bed at night embraced by the warmth of handmade quilts, and a hot water bottle at her stocking feet, she thought about what brought her here. This one singular act of betrayal gave her the crystal clarity she needed to look back on her life and enabled her to see how others might have viewed her. In all, she dismissed her younger brother and sister as being at fault for this betrayal. They were too young and did what she told them out of fear and because they could not outsmart her. She forgave her father almost immediately, because after all, she could not stay mad at him for very long anyway. Her friends did not play a part in this. They admired her. They looked upon her as something more than she really was. They treated her well because she was both beautiful and manipulative. No. It was her own mother who could be held up to the light of day and could account for shipping her off to nowhere land.

But as the days went by, as she busied herself with the demands of a small farm and slipped easily into the country company of farmers' children, Laura Mae's thoughts circled around the reasons why her mother pushed her away and pushed her out. The reason could not be hidden. She could not disguise it, nor ignore it, nor call it something that it wasn't.

Laura Mae was forced from her home because she would not obey. She could not be reasoned with, and because she had manipulated others, her siblings, her father and her friends, she had felt smug and superior to those closest to her. She refused to listen to reason, refused to do as she was asked, refused to acknowledge her own Mother as someone she should listen to and obey. She was a rebel and rebellious children, as she was forced to admit, were often given a wake-up call.

So, it did not take her long to extinguish her anger, and when she calmed down, reason poured in and took the place of her hatred. She was not so spoiled, not so full of herself to try and take it out on the sweet, small and fragile people who were her elderly grandparents. This was not their fault and she refused to punish them for what her mother chose to do. Though she was no longer angry at her mother, forgiveness was a more elusive and difficult task to master. Forgiveness requires unconditional love and Laura Mae was not sure her mother loved her at all, or ever.

Her new life offered a slightly different ambiance. Her school was small, her schoolmates simple. Though her friends admired her city clothing, she soon let go of these material things because they made her different from those dressed in simple cotton clothes. She begged her grandmother for the simple clothing that would make her blend in more. Not having to worry about being a fashion plate, she felt more comfortable with her hair pulled back in a ponytail. She wore no makeup and did not think about her nails soon after they all broke under the strain of her physically demanding chores.

She could still meet her friends at the local drugstore to share a soda, read about Hollywood stars, and go into Roseburg with no less than eight teens to watch the latest films. There were no longer any demands to maintain popularity and blending in was all that mattered. She told everyone she was sent by her Family to help her frail grandparents out because she was the oldest child. The friendships that she forged seemed more genuine and she liked people more sincerely than before. Though she was clearly the most beautiful girl in town, she did not feel the need to compete, nor was there any pressure for her to maintain appearances among this small town where everyone knew each other, and where all came together to help one another. My Mother stepped back, drew a clean breath and re-directed her life.

While it was her own mother who precipitated the plan that would inevitably change my mother's life for the better, mother would never credit her for such a good deed. My grandmother would remain harsh, demanding and unloving in support of Laura Mae for the rest of both their natural lives.

Chapter 13

Life had become a matter of routine for two young people. My Father enjoyed the work at the ranch house of "Ramona". He played tennis at the Santa Barbara racquet club and enjoyed group dates with his young friends. Free from the demands of his Uncle Jimmy and his grandfather, he embraced American life and enjoyed American freedoms.

Mother continued to help her aged grandparents, who benefited greatly from her diligence and hard work. She had many friends that were easily made in a non-assuming and unpretentious woodsy lumber town. There were no pressures for her, and the routine of farm animals and farm work stretched her personality and gave her strength and joy in her life. She no longer fought with anyone. She no longer struggled against her mother's authority. She no longer felt the need to manipulate or use others for her own gain. She was blossoming into a young, caring, and contributed young woman.

As witnessed by history, December 7, 1941 changed everything. The lives of everyone living in the United States, immigrant or American-born changed overnight with the invasion and decimation of Pearl Harbor in Hawaii. America would answer this unforgivable assault on American territory by entering World War II.

Fear entered the hearts of every American, and my mother's family was no different. They called and immediately demanded that Laura Mae come home. They left no room for questions or counter-demands. She was to return home immediately with her grandparents. Their country was at war and family needed to be close.

The answer was to give up the farm and Laura Mae would drive her grandparents back to Pasadena. A small and much more manageable house was purchased so that all could live under one roof. Togetherness, no matter what might happen, was more comforting that being apart. The grandparents gave up the familiarity and independence of farm life, and managed to live some years in the single bedroom that awaited them in Southern California. My mother threw together several essays and reports she handed in to her school in order to leave town with her graduation certificate. Reluctant to leave her friendships, she vowed to stay in touch as they drove away.

Understanding the fear and upset of her family, and her country, Laura Mae quickly found a factory job assembling crystal radio sets for the war effort. War effort jobs were becoming plentiful overnight, and the long hours prevented her from seeing much of her mother after coming home. Her mother became an expert welder and electrician under the tutelage of older male supervisors for the Lockheed plant in Pasadena. As men enlisted in the armed services, women filled jobs normally reserved for the men who were now going off to war.

My mother's younger brother, barely 18, joined the Army and was sent off to bootcamp at Fort Dix, then shipped to the Pacific theater of the war. Their new small home became an oasis for soldiers, sailors and friends who needed a place to stay temporarily before moving out. Every American did what was necessary to pitch in and support the growing war effort in both Europe and Asia. If they worked, they had money for food, gas and shelter. And though the food and gas were rationed, they did all they could to feed the less fortunate and make room for the boys who went off to war. Their unity and their efforts were truly patriotic and bonded them to a higher level of service to their country.

My mother's presence in the home roused many young men who camped in their home to their awakening emotions. It was almost laughable how many swore their dying love for my mother with the words, "make love with me tonight, because tomorrow I'll be shipped overseas, and I might not ever make it home again. Won't you give me one last moment of true happiness to remember before I die?" She became expert in pushing away their demands and defending her own honor. It wasn't easy. Soldiers, Marines, Sailors were everywhere. Every hotel was filled to overflow capacity. Many slept in lobbies or hallways. Others, like my grandparents, opened their homes to those coming and going to war. It was a different time, a scary time, but one made more manageable by unity and compassion.

It was on such occasion, when my mother found herself in the company of two other girlfriends. Each friend had a soldier or a sailor to date. My Mother had two men, one on each arm. They enjoyed the sound of the Big Bands playing at the Coconut Grove in Hollywood, and went to Chinatown in Los Angeles for a late supper. Here is where our history began.

My Father left his comfortable "House Boy" job in Santa Clarita to return to the confines of Los Angeles' Chinatown. Word had gotten out well before the mass gathering of those of Japanese descent, to return to the confines of Chinatown for their own protection. It was more than obvious that Chinese, even Chinese Americans, were not visibly different from their Japanese cousins, and the Chinese Tongs could protect you, but only if they knew where you were. It was not safe for Chinese to be outside the confines of their Chinatowns. Not only were they safe in numbers, but their restrictive boundaries could provide protection. To further provide limited protection, my father and all other Chinese, had to wear yellow "I AM CHINESE" buttons pinned to their lapels. A curfew of nine p.m. was called for by local government, and you had better be at home, or back in Chinatown, by that time, or face possible arrest or harassment by vigilante groups seeking to protect their country. While the Japanese were gathered and placed in military encampments, the Chinese, as well as other Asian groups, suffered because they could not be distinguished by the American public. For many, there was little difference between a Chinaman and a Jap. Weren't all Yellow and Brown Asian devils, foreigners who wished for the destruction of the American Way of Life? Both vigilante and local authorities alike feared what side the Chinese might choose during this war.

It was proven the night one of Dad's "cousins" was caught after curfew by a small cadre of America's "finest" who beat the piss out of him and threw his unconscious body at the Chinese gate of Chinatown. It was a warning and a testament of what waited for any one of them who stepped outside their prescribed boundaries.

It was a contributing reason the 442 regiment was formed. Known as the 442nd Regimental Combat Team (RCT), it was made up of Nisei, or second-generation Japanese volunteers from Hawaii and the mainland. Also known as the "Purple Heart Battalion," these valiant and supremely patriotic men of Asian descent suffered the most casualties during World War II.

This battalion of second-generation Japanese American-born men, known as the "Go-for-broke" fighters, was comprised of Japanese Nisei desirous of proving their loyalty to the

American Flag. They became the most decorated unit in U.S. military history for its size and length of service, simply because they had more to prove than most. They earned over 18,000 individual decorations for bravery, 9,500 Purple Hearts, and seven Presidential Distinguished Unit Citations.

My father tried to enlist in the United States Army, and was disappointed to learn that he had "flat feet". All those years standing on a wooden box as a child while pressing and ironing clothing gave him varicose veins that would haunt his entire life. He also was diagnosed with an enlarged heart from childhood Rheumatic Fever and his blood carried "malaria" contracted back in China. For him, going to war was not an option.

But Dad found easy work all over Chinatown. He did prep work in the kitchen at the Grandview Gardens restaurant, and bar-tended behind the Golden Buddha bar.

It was on such an occasion when Mom walked into his bar for the first time, with two friends and four guys in uniform. Dad kept an eye on the beautiful blue-eyed blond and her friends, while he tended the bar. He was especially attentive to her booth, giving them fresh drinks without their asking.

In the days and weeks to come, Dad recognized the beauty who graced his bar and restaurant, sometimes with different soldiers, and other times with her own family. Because the bar and restaurant stayed open very late, he was assured that no matter the late hour, she always came to the Grandview Gardens.

He was enthralled. But he knew he could not talk to her directly, not in any social manner. They were not equals, and some eager young man might wish to point that out in a threatening manner. Dad was aware of his place, and he stayed in the background and observed.

His chance finally came one evening when her dinner group

wanted to go bowling but found themselves short a "team" member. As he set fresh drinks down in front of the buoyant crowd, Mother's date asked if he bowled. "Yes," my father replied, his heart picking up speed. The invitation to accompany them to the nearby bowling alley brought my mother and Father together for the very first time. It wasn't a date, but it came close.

Soon, faces became familiar, and small friendships blossomed. My Father wanted to date her, but asking a white woman out was a very tricky venture for an Asian. For all men there was the possibility of embarrassing wholesale rejection, but for an Asian, there was the possibility of denigration as well within that same rejection. For a time, it was easier to suggest ways of meeting up with several of their small group of friends, to ensure that he was in their company, yet not alone with Laura Mae. They went bowling, of course, and boat-paddling in Los Angeles Echo Park. Baseball games and drinks and dinner at his restaurant always ensured he would see her again. What surprised him, much to his delight, was that she never refused an opportunity to get together in his company, always agreed to his suggestions for get-togethers, and seemed to gather at his side whenever "teams" were chosen. He even introduced her in the same fashion to his group of American-born Chinese friends. They seemed happy to meet the pretty blond, but their conversations were subdued and stilted whenever she came along.

Within several weeks, he gathered his courage, and during a break in conversation with yet another group of soldiers and sailors, he leaned into her, and asked her for a date, just the two of them alone.

"Would you like to go see the latest Clark Gable film with me," he whispered to her. Her head inclined toward his and she whispered, "You mean just you and me?" "Yes," came his swift reply. "Okay," she said, her head nodding in the affirmative, and back they went to their other conversations.

They arranged to meet on a specified date, and attended a daytime matinee, which was cheaper, but also allowed my Father to return to the confines of Chinatown before his designated curfew. It also guaranteed that Laura Mae would feel more comfortable in this casual meet than a real date. She took a bus to the theater, and so did he. Picking her up at her home would require him ringing her bell, and introducing himself to her Family, and that was not going to happen.

There was no attempt to hold her hand, or "yawn" and stretch his arms over his head and down around her shoulders. He made no moves toward her for a good-bye kiss, and made every attempt to make her laugh, make her feel comfortable, and make her feel special. If he could have no other experience with her, he wanted most to be a genuine friend who was counted among her good friends. He could accept that much of being part of her life, if he could not have her love.

For mother's part, she felt nervous. She liked David, and though she should never have considered this a factor, she could not deny his handsomeness. But it was his friendliness, his sense of humor and his decency toward her that made her freely accept his invitations to meet. After a while, those girlfriends closest to her noticed.

"Wow, Laura Mae! This is the third time you and that Chinaman have gone to the movies. Are you dating?"

At first, it was denial. The quickest way to avoid coming to terms with truth was to lie, and lying prevented most suspicions from growing into accusations. "No," she would tell them, "we're not dating." Don't be silly. He's a good friend of Sam's, and well, Sam can't always go when we can. He's just a friend of a friend. You know how I love the movies. No big deal."

For Dad, the course of questions and events were slightly cruder. His Chinese friends teased him mercilessly about if he "nailed the pretty white woman" yet. In their eyes, his status would be significantly increased among his peers if he had sex with a white woman pretty enough to be a Hollywood starlet. But in their eyes, and in their Society, Chinese could accept anyone having sex with a Caucasian, but loving them was forbidden. They made good whores, just don't make the mistake of falling in love. Use them, yes, but lose your heart and there would be hell to pay. That would be crossing the line and Chinese were more than aware of which side of the line they were on, and where that line was drawn in America.

My Father was fully aware of that and for some time he kept his feelings to himself. He laughed at their innuendos, and took the teasing and razzing like a brother, but his heart and the truth of what lay inside it, was hidden away secreted from the world. He dare not hope to expose it, and could not express it to anyone.

It was my bold mother who changed his mind. They had met for yet another daytime date, and as they were about to part for their respective bus stop, she hesitated, turned, and grabbed his sleeve, pulling him behind a huge palm tree trunk. There, safely hidden from the eyes of those surrounding them, she gave him a swift, unsure and unsteady kiss on the mouth, said "see you later" and ran for her approaching bus. My Father's legs would not support him, and he fell into the tree to keep him from falling to the ground. He replayed that one quick little scene over and over, until he tried to comprehend all of what it meant, and all the potential it implied. She kissed him! Not a great kiss, not a soul-kiss, but a kiss that had to mean she at least liked him. She liked him enough to kiss him. Would she let him kiss her next time? Were there kisses at all in their future, deeper, more meaningful kisses? This was a whole new world! She kissed him! And it was outdoors in broad daylight (even if behind a tree.) He wiped his mouth with a clean handkerchief and red lipstick came away with the cloth. He folded the evidence away, intending never to wash it, ever. He floated through his work week, oblivious and content in re-living every moment of that experience. He had dated one other Caucasian, but also in a casual manner, with no outward affection. It lasted for two dates and ended with her confession that her parents felt it was wrong. They never kissed. And now, his mind and imagination and heart filled in the future of this one experience with Laura Mae. He dreamed of impossible things. He finally allowed himself to at least confess to himself, and no one else, that he was falling in love with a white woman, a Gwaipo…

    Mother confessed to herself later, while riding that fateful bus home, that she didn't know why she did what she did. Everyone was chiding her not to hang out so much with David, and how awkward it was that she would still see him socially, even go to movies so often with him. She could not help herself. She liked him. But did she go too far in planting that awkward kiss on him? Why did she pull him behind the tree to do that? Would she have kissed any other man in the open, or behind a barrier against prying eyes? Was she ashamed for having kissed a Chinese man? It took a critically long time for her to calm down from her "misdeed" and to chasten herself for her outrageous conduct. Yet, try as she might, she could not deny that she wanted to kiss him. She liked him, and she wanted him to know it. David made her feel safe, and he made her feel special, and to date, none of her other suitors had evoked the same feelings. He was jovial, funny and easy to talk to. She liked his funny accent. And yes, he was Chinese, but somehow, she didn't see his Asian heritage like others did. He always smiled, and always made her laugh. She was confident in his company, and being with him, more and more actually appealed to her. Again, she struggled with herself, chastising and berating herself for having such feelings. This man was not of her race, and it was all too clear to her the damage she would cause if she continued to court this dangerous liaison.

She vowed to end their friendship the next time she saw him. He would, of course, understand that her kiss meant nothing, and their friendship was doomed. He knew she had an endless parade of young men come through their house, staying temporarily before receiving their orders to ship out. She would contrive for him a lie that she was engaged to one of them. The kiss, after all, meant nothing really.

So why, then, was she so eager to see him again?

She did not see my father for nearly two weeks, giving excuses that home and work and other friends demanded more of her time. Finally, in a rushed meeting at one in the morning, they met in the back alley of the Grandview Gardens restaurant, amidst the acrid smell of empty liquor bottles and the day's garbage. Here they could not be seen or overheard. As my father came out the door, he found Laura Mae waiting for him in the darkened alley. Without hesitation, they quickly moved into each other's arms and kissed deeply. They were lost.

In a car, or darkened theater, they would take the chance to old hands only if they were assured no one could see. On those occasions when they were emboldened in their affection for each other, they would look at each other, running away laughing at the disdainful looks of disapproving strangers. Weeks turned into months.

""What are we going to do, David?" My mother asked, her fingers lacing themselves into his. It was Fall, 1943, and a chilly wind wound through the trees above the canyon quarry.

"About what?" he responded intentionally not looking into her eyes. She, too, stared off into any direction but his.

"About us!" she declared. "What are we going to do about us?"

It was a critical question. It was a pivotal question. It hung in the air demanding a response. It was the elephant that sat between them. Finally, he sighed, and looked into her face.

"Do you want to marry me?" He asked.

Without hesitation, she responded, looking into his face. "Of course, I want to marry you. I love you."

Looking off and down the cliff side of the quarry, my father thought if he spat, he could probably hit one of those white boys below. "Then we should get married," the words came out of his mouth.

"How? How, David, do we get married?" Tears began to form in her blue eyes. "How do *we* get married?" She emphasized.

Leaning into her, he softly kissed her forehead, and simply said, "I don't know, but we'll find a way."

Chapter 14

David and Laura Mae returned to their separate lives, each keeping their pain and anguish well hidden from those around them. David stared up at the ceiling from his bed thinking and thinking, as Laura stained her pillow at night with tears she softly shed so no one would hear.

At every stolen moment they would meet, secret lovers in a world gone mad, to share what information they had learned. It was 1943 and the State of California did not permit interracial marriage. They must leave the State and find a justice of the peace who could legally bind them in matrimony. They discovered New Mexico did not have any prohibition against interracial marriage, probably because white men married Native Indians and women from across the Mexican border for many years. But how to get there? In their naivety they did not even know where New Mexico was. A library atlas explained it to them.

Father knew of one man, a trained pilot in the Army, assigned to the 442 Battalion who frequented the restaurant and bar with his Asian girlfriend who worked as a waitress in Dad's bar and restaurant. He did not know the man personally but would find out if he would fly them both, and act as a witness. Could he talk his waitress friend into coming as a witness too?

Mom thought it might be time to tell her best friend Margi and ask her to come and stand as her witness. She felt she needed one friend, one ally to help her get through this and love her despite her choices. She needed an ally.

They thought of the money they would need, they thought of dates, using a calendar to plot out days which she could excuse herself from work, tell lies to her family about leaving town with a friend, and when they both needed to return home and work. They thought of the clothing they would take, rather than buy. Buying anything remotely fancy or made for a bride or groom would attract suspicion and uninvited questions. A honeymoon was out of the question. Any attempts to take a holiday would invite suspicion from families and co-workers. They would have to take the best of the clothing they had. They sat in a great deal of silence, each wondering how they would explain to each of their Families what they did *after* they got married. The thought was filled with endless unthinkable possibilities.

They surreptitiously phoned the New Mexico courthouse in Gallup, New Mexico for information on blood tests, witnesses and procedure. They gained the name of the local justice of the peace and asked for the appropriate paperwork to be mailed to them.

Dad arranged a meeting with the waitress and her pilot friend, in a diner outside of Chinatown and in a corner booth explained to both of them what he had planned. The Asian colonel was a soft-spoken handsome man who wore civilian clothes and round dark glasses. His American-Chinese name was William Huang. While the waitress girlfriend began to squirm disapprovingly in her seat, he sat and listened quietly and intently as my father spoke. Finally, as my father sat back, finished with his narration, he leaned forward, and asked, "Do you love her enough to make a mess of your entire lives together?"

"Yes." There was no hesitation in his voice.

A moment passed as he played with his empty coffee cup.

White waitresses rarely saw need to be attentive to a table full of Orientals. "Then you both should marry. I'll do it. I can get a friend's plane, but you'll have to share the cost of the fuel front and back. It will be an honor to stand up for you at your wedding." He reached to shake my father's hand.

Grinning, my father looked at his girlfriend who was not grinning back. She was decidedly frowning. "You both crazy. I can't go with you! I get fired for having anything to do with this! And I think you crazy for loving a white woman. Who do you think you are? You and she are nuts. No business marrying white trash!" The colonel grabbed her hands to keep her still and she quieted while the flames in her eyes cooled. My Father was about to speak, when the colonel spoke his confirmation. "That's all-right David. She doesn't need to come with us, and she's right. It's better for her if it appears she knows nothing about this. She won't tell anyone, I promise you. Here's my number. Call me when you know the dates, and I'll try and arrange the plane and the flight as quickly as I can. You two better hurry because we're still at war and I'll be shipping out again soon." With that, they parted, and father hurried to tell of his good fortune and new friend.

Mom now was tasked with asking her very best friend to stand up for her, and perhaps literally hold her up at her own wedding for all the fear she held inside. She needed to trust one person, someone she felt was a true and lasting friend. Using the same tactic, she met her friend Margi for lunch at a local diner in Pasadena, and the look on her face told her friend she had something very important and very private to tell her.

"You're really in love with this guy? Hon, you sure about this? He didn't do anything to you, did he? You're not in any, well, you aren't in any 'trouble' are you, Hon?" Margi asked. It was difficult to explain it in terms Margi could understand, but finally, after much anxiety and a few tears, Margi understood. "Now, you know I can't have my best friend walking down that aisle without her best friend there to help her through it," she offered.

"Oh, it won't be a church wedding, just a simply ceremony in front of a justice of the peace," Mother clarified.

"No matter, Hon." Margi said. "I am your best friend, and I will be there for you."

With that, and promises of swearing secrecies to their plans, Mom and Margi parted with plans for a wedding on their minds.

It was agreed by the four who were a party to this secrecy to meet at the small Burbank airport at 7am on Friday, March 23, 1945. A flight plan had been registered and a small plane was fueled and wheeled out onto the tarmac.

A very nervous bride and groom to be stood holding cold hands as Colonel Huang came out of the hangar. Margi was still in the backseat trying to stay warm. The Colonel helped them unload their luggage and instructed them where to park their car, then all four boarded the tiny craft.

Not much was said during the flight. The flight alone was terrifying, let alone the thought of what they were doing or about to do. Except for Mom and Dad, all felt like strangers caught up in a very strange situation. The plane was silent except for the low roar of the single propeller engine. It was too late for words. Now was not the time for lectures or conjecture or doubts.

After landing, and securing two rooms at a small roadside motel, the girls in one, the boys in the other, they shared an equally quiet and slightly awkward dinner before retiring. Margi and Laura Mae babbled and attempts to giggle and commiserate were made before each fell quiet and sleep overtook them. The men smoked cigarettes in the dark, with one last "I hope you know what you're doing" remark from the colonel before he rolled over.

On Saturday, March 24, 1945, four neatly dressed and anxious people arrived at the county courthouse in Gallup, New Mexico. Two Asian men escorting two white women made heads turn as they walked. Two of these people were scheduled to be married in an unfamiliar State, before a judge who would not judge them. In fact, he barely looked at them. The judge took one opportunity to raise his eyes, looked at them both hard as he spoke, then lowered his eyes down at his book, and completed the short but legal ceremony. He had done this countless of times, and what was the point of telling them they were not well-suited to marry in this time and this age. To him it did not matter. He only married them. Some other judge would decide their divorce proceedings.

The honeymoon was the same motel, but a different room. The next morning, the colonel and Margi flew them down over the Rio Grande River and followed it to the Colorado River, and from there, he gave them an aerial tour of the Grand Canyon. They returned Sunday, early evening. Colonel Huang shook Father's hand and kissed Mother's cheek. He said goodbye to Margi and left them at their car. Driving in silence, they took Margi home where she got out of the car around the corner from her Parents' house to avoid attracting their attention.

There was a small hotel in Hollywood, clean, affordable and where they did not ask questions. Laura Mae had reserved a single bedroom a week ago under her name, and as David held her bags, the desk clerk only assumed he was a driver helping her with her bags. They had returned to the real world, and that meant they could not get a room together without the threat of being denied and kicked out.

Tomorrow they would both tell their people what they did. Expecting they would be kicked out; they had arranged for alternative housing. If Laura Mae could not stay in her room until a place could be found to rent, Margi agreed to let her stay with her in her bedroom. She would naturally lie to her parents about the marriage, but that would give Laura Mae time to find a place to live. Dad had a cousin he could safely bunk with until they could find a rental of their own.

Times were that rentals in Los Angeles County were difficult to find and rented at a premium. Apartments were rare, and private citizens were opening their homes and spare rooms and garages to soldiers and those working in war-effort factories and businesses. The newlywed couple would have to live apart until they could find a place of their own. Chinese were not allowed to buy property in California, nor rent property outside of Chinatown without business agreements. It wasn't known how long this might take because Dad was still confined to Chinatown by the imposition of the war-time county curfew.

I can't explain what transpired as each confessed their secrets to their families. Mother shed tears, choking on her sobs as she defended herself against the rage of her mother, the disbelief of her wounded father, and her sister who refused to make sense of anything. What would this do to her younger brother, now fighting for his country in the Philippines? Their very patriotism would be questioned by all who knew them if they embraced this marriage. For God's sake, what will the neighbors think parading a Chinaman for a husband? It went on for hours and days. When a sense of calm descended, it was like a weighty pall over the household. Days later, it was agreed that Laura Mae could stay until they could find another place to move.

Her Mother begged her not to tell any of their friends or neighbors, and she was never to bring him to their house. "No one must know, Laura Mae! No one!" she petitioned. The shame she brought to them was obvious.

My Father's confession was more fearful. He had long removed himself from the daily threats of his Uncle Jimmy who now worked in Northern California. But his Uncle Shorty was here in Los Angeles Chinatown and had direct phone contact with his father in Salinas and his younger brother in Oakland. They would be told, and Shorty did not want to be the one to tell them what David had done. He figured if he scared some sense into him, that he would just leave the white woman alone. So, not being a smart man, but a bold one, he sent four "cousins" over to Dad's room to "shake him up a little." They woke him with a hard thump to his metal bed frame as they burst through his bedroom door, each armed with a stick of wood. They jumped him as he lay in his bed and held him fast as he struggled against them. They hit him with their sticks, not hard enough to break bones, but hard enough to bruise. "Leave the White Trash alone, Cousin, or you be in big trouble next time we come!" They left as quickly as they came. Their message was short and only slightly painful.

Father sat at the edge of his bed, rubbing his arms and legs, and wondering what the hell just happened. Feeling as though he did all he could to discourage the young whelp, Uncle Shorty made a call to Harry and his brother Jimmy. "Yeah! I beat the hell out of him. Told him to leave the White Devils alone. No! She doesn't live here with him." With that, no decision was made except to make all efforts to keep them apart, if possible.

In the ensuing days and weeks that followed, both my young newlywed parents discovered that not only were rentals scarce, but no one would dare rent to two people, married or not, of disparate races. *"I will not rent to Orients!" "Asians are not allowed." "They should be in camps or deported." "Honey, you can't be serious. You married a what?"*

This sums up the battle they fought just to find a room with a kitchenette to set up their first home together. On one occasion, weary from the onslaught of bigotry and incredulity, Mother came upon an apparent sweet woman who had converted her stand-alone garage at the rear of her enormous house into a small apartment. The woman, dressed in a cotton dress of bright red, with pearls at her neck, soft chestnut hair and ruby red lips was pleased to show her around the tiny, but tastefully done space. Returning to the main house, the woman asked Mother encouragingly to sit and tell her about her new husband. "You must be still nervous, you're such a young bride. Is your man in the military?" The woman stepped forward and handed Mother a cup of tea served in a beautiful set of bone China patterned with little purple pansies. Mother took a deep breath, and explained the nature of her marriage and husband. Expecting tea and China to start flying in rage, Mother held her breath looking down at the floor. The woman hesitated, and then replied in her kindest voice. "You poor sweet thing! You must be having a horrible time finding a place to live. I think I can help you!" Mother's eyes flew up and a smile squirmed at the edges of her mouth. Something like hope welled up inside her chest. "My brother is an attorney here in Los Angeles, and he can get you… oh! What do you call them? Oh, yes! An annulment." The woman got up and crossed the room, talking to Mother as she went. "Now, you wait here, and I'll find you his business card (Oh, bother! Where did I put those things?) You get a divorce, Darling, and I'll rent that space to you, no problem!"

As the woman returned, her brother's business card in her

hand, she saw that my mother left in a hurry, leaving the tea cup overturned on her now wet and stained pretty petit-point footstool.

In the end, they finally found a two-bedroom apartment, where a single Asian woman lived over a Chinese storefront inside the perimeter of Los Angeles' Chinatown district. A Chinese lawyer had a practice in the office space below, and above rooms were let to Asians only. When my father explained to the Chinese landlord that he had a Caucasian bride, the old man merely shrugged and said the apartment was to be shared with a young girl who worked at a publishing house downtown. "Pay your rent. No pets. No noise. No police," warned the proprietor. It was all he said.

For the moment, this would solve the dilemma of having to stay within the confines of Chinatown during the war and gave them a place to live independent of both their families.

It took another series of arguments before Laura Mae could leave her parent's home for good. "How can you, a white woman, live in Chinatown, will you tell me that?" her mother screamed at her. "You love these Chinks so much you want to live among them, is that it?" The words, the threats, the pain of everything that was said died away as she grabbed her last bag, walked out and closed the door of her family home one last time.

Chapter 15

Their new roommate was named Sun Yin Woo. She was twenty-four years old, a product of Kowloon, Hong Kong who accompanied her parents to California when she was eighteen. Her parents once lived and worked in Chinatown. Her father passed away a year ago, and her mother moved to live with her single sister in San Francisco. Sun Yin's English was very good, almost too proper. She was quiet and demure in the traditional oriental sense leaving you to wonder what really was going on inside her head. She never said, and spoke gently, responding to questions in short, but well-mannered words. Her room was across from theirs, with a small kitchenette and living room combination between them. They had to share one very tiny bathroom. All the walls, the doors, the cupboards were painted an unpleasant industrial green as though no other paint was available in the whole of the world. Only the floors broke the color scheme by daring to be dark wood. There was one single light fixture that hung low over the small dining table that had four mis-matched wooden chairs. The stove had a small oven with three small gas burners on top which had to be lit with wooden matches. The kitchen counters were also green, and perhaps served as the inspiration for the color of the walls and doors. In front of the kitchen table sat a very worn horsehair rose colored sofa and two unremarkable wooden end tables with only one lamp between them. The only cheery thing worth mentioning of the space was the bright yellow kitchen curtain that sported bright daisy flowers against a farmer's fence in a country field scene with a barn and a tractor in the background. If you stared at it long enough, it gave you a sense of the outdoors, far away from city life and this hovel of a room.

Sun Yin needed to catch an early bus to work and was the first to rise. She was ultra-quiet and gone without notice for the most part. When Mom and Dad arose to start their day, it felt as though the apartment was theirs alone for a while. Mom cooked breakfast and made coffee for Dad, which he was not in the least grateful for. It felt strange, and too American. He was not used to toast and eggs or bacon for breakfast, and ate it only grudgingly until he told her one day that he wasn't a big breakfast eater. Mom adjusted. All parties reassembled in their tiny space each evening they did not find themselves doing other things. A bargain was struck to save money on food by sharing dinners on most weekdays, and on weekends to everyone's mutual appetites. This was short-lived.

Sun Yin, they learned, ate like a bird, and preferred Chinese food. Mother did not know the first thing about cooking Chinese cuisine, and barely had knowledge of food beyond the basics of toast, eggs and bacon. She once watched in horror as Sun Yin prepared a bit of rice and boiled chicken feet for her dinner. At this point, Mom and Dad ate out at local cafes a great deal of the time, or Mom sat alone and ate at the Grandview Gardens restaurant while Dad tended the bar patrons. Sun Yin was happy to eat her boiled chicken feet and a bit of tofu in her broth alone and in sweet silence.

Life settled into a smooth-running routine, and the roommate arrangement felt amicable and supportive. Sun Yin never questioned their marriage. Never asked why they would do something like this and never proffered a word of discouragement or bigotry. She simply did not judge them in ways that could be seen or felt.

On the streets of Chinatown, locals did not dare to question a white woman, but finding it curious that she was seen in the company of my Father so frequently, native tongues wagged behind her back, and soon, it was well understood in their small community that Father had married outside his race. It was after this, Mother learned she could not shop in any grocery store within Chinatown, nor was she welcomed to engage any local in conversation. They simply ignored her and refused her trade. Knowing she did not speak Chinese, many locals took to yelling at her, curses and threats she could not understand. When they stooped to pick something up, anything up from the ground to hurl at her, she understood all too well the contempt they had for her. Her routine was to always shop outside of Chinatown before returning to their small apartment, and closing out the world whenever she closed their door.

Father stayed well away from his Uncle Shorty, knowing that his threats and conversations only centered around the white woman he brought to Chinatown. His kinder cousins warned him that Shorty was in no mood, and to stay the hell away. He had heard that his grandfather and Uncle Jimmy were also aware of his marriage, and he did not wish to risk any confrontation with either of them. He worked at the bar and met his wife outside Chinatown at their usual cafe, before returning home to the confines of Chinatown.

They soon stopped acting like a couple outside their apartment. They confessed to no one they were married. If no one asked, no one was told the truth, and neither would have to contemplate the onslaught of derision and scoffs or lectures that might await them. They simply learned not to offer any information about the other spouse if they could possibly avoid it. It meant that they did not attend parties or gatherings. They did not socialize with others. Their lives were confined to work, their apartment and each other generally away from the eyes of those who would judge them. It was a life of isolation, and they took to it as the best alternative to utter chaos. For Mother, she lost the celebration of being married. She could not find a release of her joy in her new husband. There simply was no one to celebrate openly with, except little Sun Yin.

However, on one occasion, they found themselves all sharing an impromptu meal around their little dining table, and as they ate in appreciation, Sun Yin spoke up in unusual fashion. "I, too, have a forbidden love," she spoke softly, her eyes cast down to her plate. My Mother spoke first, "What did you say?"

"There is a man at work, my boss. We are in love. For a long time now, we love each other," came her reply.

Mom and Dad looked at each other, then back at the small Asian girl. No one said anything to her, so she continued. "It is a forbidden love, because we cannot declare ourselves like you have. He is married. He has three children. His father owns the company and would disown him. We love a long time now."

Mom reached over to Sun Yin and placed her hand lovingly on her arm. The gesture that came with no words told Sun Yin that she understood her plight and sympathized. Sun Yin only sat, taking another bite of her meal as tiny pools of tears filled her lower eyelids.

Life had to remain simple, for their lives were complicated enough. The summer months were stifling inside their dark apartment, and as the days grew longer, it was more pleasant to return to their cool hiding place above the stone quarry in the San Gabriel mountains after work. They brought sandwiches and fruit and ate atop the quarry most evenings. They stayed outdoors if they could before returning home. During these summer days and nights, Sun Yin was barely seen about the place.

On the war front, great and terrible things were happening, and with the creation and deployment of two hydrogen atom bombs, the War with Japan was coming to an end. Each day the radio was filled with reports of defeats and victories. Newspaper headlines graphically displayed the horrors and atrocities of Hiroshima and Nagasaki in banner headlines. By July, politicians and world leaders were taking credit for bringing this part of the world war to an end. Cities, the Japanese internment camps, and, indeed, the country were preparing for the ending of the second world war. It was August 1945.

David and Laura's young lives were about to change once again.

Chapter 16

They were surrounded by chaos in the hot August sun as the war with Japan came to an end. It wasn't long after that the county curfews were lifted all over the country. There was hope again of finding their own place to live, though the search would be just as difficult as before. Mom tolerated living within Chinatown, but she knew she was not a welcomed sight. She enjoyed the quiet, unseen nature of young Sun Yin, but the sights and smells of that tiny apartment did not give her a sense of "home". But the thought of knocking on doors seeking another place to live among her own kind also frustrated her heart. She was reluctant to invite the bigotry she expected each time she would explain her marriage to others.

Shortly after the end of the War, and before the chaos of returning soldiers began to change the workforce in America, a plot was devised to separate and dissolve this marriage once and for all.

Uncle Shorty left word with my father that an urgent call from his grandfather was left with him. David was to call him as soon as he could. To assuage his doubt and suspicion, the messenger added that it was good news, happy news. It only served to confuse him even more.

Staring at the ceiling one night, in bed, Laura and David wondered how it could be possible that Harry would have any good news for the grandson that was not his grandson, and one who had married a "white devil." Before turning over for the night, Mom kissed him and said, "We don't need him in our lives, so just ignore the message."

With those words, the plot escalated.

Dad did as Mother suggested and ignored the message to call Harry. A month had passed, and Laura and David were having an al fresco dinner in their favorite park. The romance was still evident in their relationship, and if they could avoid strangers willing to pronounce judgments on them, they enjoyed brief moments of affection and joy in public. On this occasion, Mother squeezed Father's hand in hers well enough to cause him to turn his gaze upon hers. She lingered, hesitant and a bit unsure.

"What?" Came his response to her hesitant silence.

"How would you feel," she said slowly and then stopped.

"What is it?" He asked impatiently, giving her hand a squeeze of confidence in return.

"Oh! I'll just say it," she said, looking around to ensure their privacy. "David, I'm pregnant. We're going to have a baby."

He took the requisite few seconds to allow her words to register on the Daddy ears he had yet to form. "Pregnant?"

"A baby!" He said a bit too loudly, enough to make Mother look around her again. "We're going to have a baby!"

The hugs, the tears, the laughing and the kissing, in this very public place, were a mini-celebration of their lives, and the new life yet to come into this world. Nothing, at this one moment was wasted on the world around them, and nothing could stop their infinite love.

In actuality, though she showed a little, Mother was now five months pregnant and due to give birth in February 1946, a mere four months away. She had waited to tell Father of her pregnancy after she had saved enough money to be examined by a doctor. Though they had no way of knowing, the child would be a girl, and she would be small, as fragile and tiny as a China doll.

Pending her due date, both agreed to work as many extra hours they could and to be frugal in their existence to save money for the hospital and delivery. No more eating out, and no more funds for movies and other luxuries. If they worked hard, they could have only half the money they needed to ward off the debt of childbirth. In their focus about how to save money, or perhaps borrow money from those they knew, Mom and Dad had completely forgotten the message to call his Grandfather Harry.

Harry decided to make the decision easier for Dad. The rumor of a pending baby reached his ears from Los Angeles, and he pondered. To lure him to his trap, he must have bait.

In an unlikely move, Harry visited a realtor who showed him a small house with two bedrooms in the suburbs of Salinas not far from the downtown area and surprised the realtor by pulling out cash closing the purchase he made in his business' name. Then he called Shorty and told him to speak to the owner of the Grandview Gardens and have Dad fired from his job.

In a very short time, a dejected father-to-be came home to tell Mom and Sun Yin that he had been summarily dismissed for no reason that could be figured out. As planned, before he could figure out their next move, and without time to grieve over the loss of his job, the phone down the hall was heard ringing. The manager always answered the phone because he generally knew if tenants were home or not. It surprised Mom and Dad that he knocked at their door and spoke through the door that the phone was for them. No one ever called for them here. Mom and Dad both went to the phone, both curious, both concerned. Phone calls were not likely to be good news.

As my father lifted the receiver to his ear and said 'hello' the caller was immediately identified as Chinese and spoke in his native tongue. The caller was Harry himself, and my father's neck stiffened, and Mom felt his tension.

"Grandson," Harry declared. "David. Are you there?"

"Yes, this is he," Dad responded in Chinese.

"I greet you, my son, and offer peace between us, you and I." His voice was filled with warmth and a bit of humility, or so Dad thought. "I know there has not been peace between you and I for many years, but I still consider you to be my grandson. You are my Family despite our differences and our history together. I call you to offer my peace and to invite you to come back."

"What do you mean 'come back'?" asked my father cautiously.

"You know that we have many businesses to operate. All my five sons are quite busy with their own restaurants and laundry houses. I myself have more than I can handle with my gambling houses and my working girls. I have a new restaurant that I am opening and have no one to operate it. I know of your work at the Grandview, and I want you to quit your job and come work this restaurant for me. I will give you 70 percent ownership, and I will take only 30 percent for my share of the business." Harry's voice was bright with promise.

"Grandfather, I have a pregnant wife, and…" Father spoke.

"Yes! Yes. A wife, and now a child comes. Yes! You must have a house then, too. I have a small two-bedroom house, and I will provide help for your pregnant wife. I will pay all medical expenses for you until you build up this business. Until you get settled on your own financially. It will be a good enterprise, my Grandson."

"A house? And you will cover our medical expenses?" Father spoke in English so Mother would understand. Her eyes grew large at the mention of these gifts, and then she grew suspicious. She whispered into his other ear, "What does he want in return?"

"Grandfather," my father was hesitant to emphasize, "You know of my wife, do you not?"

"Yes, yes! Of course. Not my choice, but this is America, and we must accept that you can do these things in a free country. Yes, yes! With a baby, you will need a stable income, and a house and to be close to Family again. I have many things you can help me out with, and your wife can find work also, if she wishes to work."

Father lowered the receiver, and held his hands over it, as he turned to Mother and said, "I can't believe it! The old man wants me to quit my job here and run one of his restaurants. He has a house for us and he's going to pay all of our medical bills when the baby comes! He says he's forgiven us for marrying and said you can work for him, too!"

Mother's jaw dropped, and she felt faint. "I don't believe it!"

Back on the phone again, he said: "Grandfather, excuse my ignorance. But you want me to quit my job here, move up to Salinas and take over one of your restaurants…"

"A small cafe, really," he interrupted, "but it sits off the highway and does a brisk trade."

"And you will give us a house and pay for our medical expenses, too?"

"Yes, of course, Grandson. I need your help. You are necessary to help our family, and you and your new bride are family and we must help each other. Forgive an old man and come up here. I need you, my son. Come help an old man."

"How soon would you need us?" asked my father as he began to show excitement in his body.

"How soon can you quit your job at Grandview?" asked his grandfather.

"That won't be a problem," came Dad's reply.

"Then do you have enough money to move up here? The

house is ready, and it may take me a week to get some furniture in there for you, but come... come ahead. Two weeks, and we shall be ready for you."

"Two weeks! Yes! Yes, Grandfather. Thank you. Thank you. You don't know how great your timing is." Yes, we will see you in two weeks!"

There was a series of goodbyes, and then my father hung up and grabbed his wife with both hands. He danced her around. Since the entire conversation was in Chinese, Laura was still confused. He repeated the entire conversation for her.

"Aha! Everything is going to be fine now. In two weeks, we will have our own place to live, our own house! I will be owner of my first restaurant, and we will have income, and we won't need to worry about medical expenses for our baby!

"David, are you sure about this? What would make that old man turn around and embrace the both of us? I thought you said he hated white people with a purple passion?" Laura Mae asked.

"No... no! You're married to me now. He still considers me his grandson and even though I'm not really, he wants me to be part of the family. He's getting old. He needs my help. The timing couldn't be better! We're free, and we can move out of Chinatown to a new life together."

He read the hesitation and doubt in her face. "C'mon, Laura! Do this for me. Do this for us. I promise to always protect you, but I really think this is going to work out fine. Trust me, Honey. We're on our way!"

He grabbed her and whirled her off her feet. She held on as though there would be no tomorrow.

Chapter 17

Salinas Valley was not the big city, or anything near it. Coming through the old Highway 99, they passed field after field, row after row of vegetables and fruit orchards. They even stopped at a roadside fruit stand and bought a wooden carton of strawberries smelling of sunshine, earth and sugar.

They had a little goodbye party in their apartment on a Friday evening just as Sun Yin returned from work. She was sad at their leaving and worried about who would replace them as a roommate. She told them in her usual quiet fashion that she enjoyed their company more than anyone else who had lived there. As Father said goodbye and gave her an awkward hug, he left the room. Mom sat Sun Yin down and gently told her of her feelings about her boss, their affair and how useless it was to believe he would leave his wife in the end for her.

"Oh, no! I agree. He will never divorce his wife to marry me." Then why pursue such a futile and unhappy relationship my mother questioned. "We are…" she hesitated. "We are like the movies and books say, 'Star-Crossed Lovers.' There is no hope for us in the end."

Mom pursued the line of questioning and asked if she wanted to be happy, to be married and to have children someday. "Yes, and I will have all those things, but I love him now and always, no matter who I choose to marry in the end. It cannot be helped, and I cannot deny our forbidden love."

Mother felt awful, and certain her boss did not feel the same as Sun Yin. To her, it was obvious that he was using the poor girl because he could. Feeling herself getting angry at the frustration of it, Mother wanted to find out the wife's name and leave a phone call before she left town and see how long the illicit love affair would last. But knowing this was not any of her business, and not wanting to hurt her fragile little friend more, she gathered herself in silence, gave Sun Yin a tight squeeze, and said goodnight. The next morning about five o'clock they rose up, finished packing their sedan and said goodbye to Sun Yin and Los Angeles.

The few hours it took to reach Salinas gave both Mom and Dad an opportunity to think and talk of what lay ahead. For Dad, it held out a hand of hope on several levels. He was given a chance to be taken back as a family member, including his wife, and in reconciliation with his grandfather, he would help to run one of his businesses. He felt confident in running a restaurant, having participated in the kitchen and cooking industry through his cousins and uncles. This business meant more income at a time when starting a family demanded more income. He was sure Laura Mae would not have to work at all, and only if she wanted to, making him the breadwinner and provider, as it should be, he thought. And while they were getting on their feet, they would not have to worry about finding housing, being ignored, threatened or harassed by bigoted landlords and though they had not seen the house, they could live in a real neighborhood, in a real house they could call home. Father was feeling that, at last, he could provide for his wife and coming Family, and be part of a real community that hopefully would accept him as a good man. The war was over, to some degree, Orientals were no longer the enemy (or at least as enemies they were soundly defeated) and Father knew how prosperous his grandfather was in Salinas

Valley. This could mean a great deal of success.

Mother's thoughts were not so full of hope. She was scared. Of course, David had told her horror stories about his childhood, the child labor that was also slave labor and how they treated him in the past. Why, suddenly, would these people start being nice, offer a home, to pay their medical bills and give him a restaurant to run? It raised the hairs on the back of her neck just thinking of it, and this meant her instincts were guarded and suspicious. Yet here she was almost two months from giving birth to her first-born child and no way to pay for it. She reconciled her thoughts with the thought of having her own home. It was not an apartment, not a converted garage, not a basement, nor an attic. This was a real two-bedroom, one bath, full kitchen, dining room and living room, with a detached garage and a yard front, back and side of the house. She asked David if it had a fireplace, but he did not know.

Harry's instructions were to pick up the keys to the house at the real estate agent's office, and after getting somewhat settled, come to the restaurant for a meal and introductions. That part gave Laura Mae flutters in her stomach. The stories of this man created a tyrannical image of a very strong, very big, and very abusive Chinese man. How would she possibly eat a meal in front of that?

The realtor was gracious and acted unsurprised as Mom and Dad entered his office asking for the key to the house on 211 Archer Street. He told them a little of their neighborhood, showing them on a map how to get to the house, where the grocery store and filling station was, and where the elementary school was when the time came. Excited, the two left with keys, smiles and handshakes, and eagerly returned to their car.

The house was easy to spot. The realtor's sign was still

posted on the window, with a "sold" sticker over it. It was a white clapboard farm home, with a wide expansive porch painted grey. Paver steps led to the front porch and a bare bulb stood at the top of the door frame looking in need of a cover. A tree large enough to provide some shade on hot days stood off center on the front lawn. Two large window panes, with smaller window panels above served as the home's eyes on the world. They looked around, and saw no neighbors outside the tree-lined neighborhood. Only seven other small homes graced this one small, short dead-end street, and all were nicely spaced with about 30 feet or more between them. They quickly and nervously unlocked the front door, holding the wooden screen door with their hips, and let it slam behind them as they entered. The sound of the soft "wham" was theirs now.

  They both stood still, breathing in the dust and odors, letting the view of the rooms sink in: a small living room to the right, a dining room to the left, a glimpse of a kitchen to the back of the house, a short hallway. There was a gas furnace with a wall thermostat. The floors were a light oak wood with stains. The walls were painted a butter yellow, except the dining room which had a white floral-patterned wallpaper with shades of green and brown. They walked slowly through and found a small, white-tiled bathroom with chrome fixtures. Across from the bathroom was one large bedroom, and further down the hall, a much smaller one that had a single very old metal bed frame still in it. The kitchen was the cheeriest room, catching the sun's rays through two large windows, one over the sink and one that served as their eating area that held a convenient but small vinyl booth and table. The counters were mostly a built-in drain board on one side of the sink and a smaller counter on the other. Sweet and small tiered shelving flanked the large kitchen window over the sink, and no curtains were hung. Hopes of picking out and sewing her own curtains elevated the moment. Laura Mae laughed. The floor was three different kinds of floor linoleum, as though one could not make up their minds, or else had used scraps of leftovers given away for free. Somehow, it didn't much detract from the joy both felt as they admired each room and absorbed the character of the house. Father was already out the back door, surveying the long, narrow yard filled with uncontrolled weeds and grass standing next to a sad-looking garage with moss on its roof due to the tree that grew right next to it. "Honey, I think we have a fruit tree here," he shouted as she peered out the window at him.

It was hard to hold down the excitement. Thoughts of furniture, furnishings, colors, paint flew through their heads, along with thoughts of dread, tempered with 'this isn't really ours.' They knew they ought to tamp down their excitement with the possibility of failure, and having to move on if things with his grandfather did not work out. But now, this very moment, they rushed into each other's arms and danced and laughed and yelled, giving themselves one honest, genuine moment of happiness before reality took over their senses again.

They had saved furiously for the baby while in Los Angeles and managed to save almost a thousand dollars. It was hoped they could use that money to help furnish their house as long as they could confirm their grandfather's desire to pay for their forthcoming medical bills. They would ask this directly when they met with him later in the day. For now, they worked at unloading their few belongings from the car into the palace they wanted to call 'home'.

At 5pm that early evening, a phone rang inside the house. It rang continually, as both Laura and David searched for it. It was found inside a cupboard in the hallway. It was an old-fashioned stand up with a receiver on a hook at the side. Mother was delighted as most phones now were the heavy black cradle Bakelite phones with the large dials. This was, indeed, an old house. She lifted the receiver and said 'hello'. When she heard Chinese spoken, she almost dropped the phone as she quickly passed it to David like a hot potato burning her hands. The conversation proceeded in his strange dialect, and she fell back and away from it, returning to hang up her clothing in their bedroom closet. Dad entered the bedroom shortly after the conversation ended.

"Grandfather wishes to meet us both at his restaurant. It's the restaurant I will be running for him. He's anxious to meet you."

"David," she said, shaking out a blouse and reaching for a wire hanger, "I don't look forward to this. I don't understand why he's being so nice to us all of a sudden."

"I know. I know. But let's reserve judgment until we have a chance to meet and see what his plans are. Maybe it's really true he needs us to help him out now that Jimmy is up in Oakland. He's here alone, and he can't run everything himself."

Without saying the words, Dad was hoping that this might be the breaking in to a real Family that he always wanted and always needed. Perhaps Harry could appreciate him, his work, his input and help, and finally accept him as part of his Family. He was certainly willing to find out and even willing to forgive the past, if he could just be forgiven and taken back in the family fold.

Harry's plans were falling into place just as he had hoped. He realized his grandson was still naive enough to trust his word, and therefore, he could be manipulated. He was satisfied that all was going to work out.

He had bought this restaurant many months ago with the idea of adding its income to his local enterprises. As always, his gambling houses and prostitutes brought in a steady stream of business. Except for paying off the local sheriffs, the money, combined with the steady incomes from his five sons and their businesses, gave Harry a comfortable lifestyle, plenty of cash and the feeling of power he craved. This restaurant did a fair business, but as Harry viewed it, it could do better. The cook/owner was a tired man, having first cooked for the United States Navy, then cooked on a merchant ship. This small business of his was his only reality before retirement. The food was so-so, the waitresses, including his aging wife, were frumpy and cranky, and the trade were regular townsfolk with a sprinkling of Hispanic and Chinese field workers and the occasional folk from Highway 99. Harry offered up a sizeable sum that made the aging mariner blink with possibilities. He took the money without hesitation, agreed to run the business until new management could be hired, and bought fishing brochures for fishing spots in Idaho. The cook's previous owner put his house up for sale, and while pending, he and the missus kept their eyes on a silver streamline trailer that offered every latest luxury in motor home convenience.

Harry sat at the middle booth alone, watching the entrance door carefully between sips of his coffee. It would not be difficult to spot his grandson despite the intervening years. He would be the one accompanied by a pregnant white woman. Harry practiced his fake smile, but inside he chuckled for another reason.

David and Laura walked in, both sets of eyes sweeping the room, sizing up their surroundings, and spotted Harry right away.

They walked over to his table and stood, until Harry jumped up and said, "Sit! Sit."

Sliding into the opposite side of Harry's booth, Harry motioned to the waitress. "Madge! Two more coffees here!" he said in funny English. Turning to Mom, he asked, "Would you, dear lady, like anything else? Tea or Coca-Cola perhaps?"

Barely able to look into his face, she shyly replied, "No, coffee would be just fine." David offered her a cigarette, which she took immediately, just to keep her nervous hands busy. Madge brought the coffees and refilled Harry's cup at the same time.

"We will order some food in a while. Let us get acquainted. David, your wife here is a beauty of a woman – such blue eyes!" he crowed.

"Grandfather, I'd like to introduce you to my wife, Laura," Father offered.

"Laura; Laura," his grandfather repeated. It gave my mother the shivers as he tried to pronounce the "L" and failed. It sounded more like "Roar-ra."

"Laura," he continued. "You like my grandson, yes?"

"I- I love your grandson," Mom replied.

"Yes, yes, you do," Harry's smile almost appeared painful. "Family is important, yes? Of course. Two people in love, now a family. Yes, yes! But David has other Family, and we don't always get along, but nevertheless, family is family. We need David. His family need him. We need both you and David. You like the house, Laura?" He continued to strain her name like he was mashing it through a sieve.

Laura looked at her husband, and David replied, "The house is great, grandfather. It's really swell of you to provide for us like this. What must we do to repay you?"

"Repay? No, no repay. Just work for me, help me run my business here. I cannot run everything alone, see? Look around. This good business place. Lots of customers. Food bland, need better cook, more menu, then people come better. More people mean more money. You help?" Harry's words spilled like an open faucet.

Mom and Dad surveyed the small café and found the set up pleasant. The dark brown booths and the counters were in very good shape, the white tile floor was clean, and the chrome behind the counters shined and reflected back the lighting from the pendant ceiling lights. The walls could stand some fresh paint, and Mom immediately thought ruffled curtains would cheer up the décor, but in all, the space was cozy, workable, mostly clean and operative. Two waitresses, both in their late fifties or early sixties were dressed in identical tan uniform dresses, with white ruffled, highly starched caps and a huge, flowered handkerchief pinned to their right shoulders. Their white highly starched aprons matched their white hose and white shoes. They not only looked alike, but both wore their pencils above their left ear, and sported what looked to be the same red lipstick.

"Can I check out the kitchen, grandfather," my father asked. Mother made a grab for his hand as he began to rise. He sat back down, and whispered into her ear, "I'll be back in a second. You'll be all right." He got up and headed for the kitchen, leaving Laura to puff on her cigarette and look down at her coffee cup.

"Yes, yes!" Harry said, feeling compelled to keep conversation flowing. "Laura is a pretty name for a pretty woman. Glad she married David. Glad she here. Ah! When baby due?"

Mother's eyes came up to his. "Our baby is due in two more months, at the middle or end of February."

"Boy or girl baby?" Harry smiled at her.

"Oh, it doesn't matter to me, as long as it's healthy, you know, ten fingers, ten toes," Mother offered.

"No, no! In China, first-born baby must be boy. First one must be boy. You have boy, Laura," he struggled with her name making it sound like it had more than two syllables. "Good for you, good for family."

Father returned and sat down. "Looks simple enough, though I think he could use some help in the kitchen, Grandfather."

"Yes, yes, need all new help here. Get rid of elderly waitresses. Hire young females. Laura! You be waitress after baby birth, yes! Hire new cooks, better menu. Here." He tossed menus in front of Mom and Dad. "See. Food simple. Awful, no flavor. You see. Order some food. We eat now. You see."

Both Mom and Dad agreed. The food was basic. The dinner had three choices of fried chicken with mashed potatoes and vegetable, liver and onions with mashed potatoes and vegetable and steak with mashed potatoes and vegetable. Father's quick tour of the kitchen saw the mashed potatoes fixed early and put on a steam table to keep warm and the vegetables consisted of canned green beans also warmed by the same steam table. The cooks had only to deep-fry chicken or grill a steak or liver with some onions to be done. The waitresses added biscuits and butter, and pies of questionable homemade skills were offered as dessert for ten cents a slice. They decided to order one of everything so they could sample the flavors of each dish to determine the merit of each. After their meal, much was left uneaten. Harry and David, of course, did not favor American food. Laura did not think anything had enough seasoning and understood why Harry called it bland.

"Grandfather, with the right cook, we could double the menu size, offer more proper dishes. We could offer fish, salads, rice, more vegetable choices, more flavor choices. We could make way better desserts. We could put in an ice cream freezer and make milkshakes and sundaes and offer fountain drinks! We can put in a jukebox – you know – big band music so that young people will want to hang out here, too." Father's face lit up with each new idea keeping pace with his enthusiasm.

"Ah! See! Good ideas. Good ideas, Grandson. Good. You know how to run this place then?" Harry asked.

"I watched carefully how business is done at Grandview Gardens and at Uncle Shorty's restaurant. I know how to cook some dishes. 'I am learning all the time. If we can hire a real good cook, he can teach me all he knows, and we can double… hell! We could triple this business!" Dad was fairly jumping in his seat.

Harry bowed his head. "Yes. Yes." He crooned softly. "Yes. Yes. You good boy, David." He reached into his jacket pocket and pulled out a stack of bills. Here is two thousand. Mother's eyes flew open wide, staring at the wad of money. Harry continued. You interview and hire good cook. You hire young, pretty waitresses, you buy what you need here. Keep receipts. Keep books for me. Open new restaurant in thirty days. Thirty days, you open and I come back. Show me success, and I keep you. In thirty days good, you stay. If not, you go. Yes?"

Mom and Dad sat still for a moment, and then Dad said, "Yes, Grandfather. I will give you a great business in thirty days' time." This part of the conversation was in Cantonese.

Mother looked first at David, then at Harry, and leaned in with her question, "What about…" She was nervous. "What about our baby? You promised to pay our medical bills, too. Is that true, Grandfather?"

Father thought she should not be so bold, but before he could quiet her, Harry responded, a new smile stretched his face. "Of course, my pretty lady. I will pay hospital bills. I have a Chinese doctor in town. I give you name and phone number. You see him. He good doctor. Good man. All paid for. You work for me, I pay you. I give you house. I watch over you like Family. Yes? Good? Good, good. You need furniture? Yes, furniture – you buy, I pay for all. You need a bed to sleep, yes? Not to worry. Not to worry," he told them.

Harry reached out for Mom's hand and cupped it in his. "You must call me Grandpa Harry. Grandpa Harry," he repeated for her. He stood now, bowing and smiling as he moved out of the booth.

Before he turned to leave, he whispered in Chinese to David, "You come alone to my place on 7484 Main Street. Come tomorrow at 11 am. We talk details." Harry left with his fists clenched. How long must I endure this, he wondered as he climbed into his sedan and drove off.

David and Laura made themselves as comfortable as possible on the floor of their new bedroom, in their new house. The day's events played out before them over and over, until they fell into a natural sleep holding onto each other.

Chapter 18

The days and weeks flew by. Father left Mother alone for the better part of each day as he drove from Salinas down to Los Angeles and back again getting all he needed for the Grand Opening of his new restaurant. While he was researching, he agreed to pay the owner to stay open two more weeks, leaving him only two weeks to paint, re-decorate and set up the place as his own. Every evening, he and Mother met over a rushed meal to compare notes and check off lists and make even more lists in preparation.

Their excitement built and fed off each other. Laura shopped for materials for new window curtains. David found a refurbished juke box and a used grill with larger ovens. They decided on a cream-colored paint with red checkered curtains that complimented the existing vinyl booths and counter stools. The flooring would have to do until more funds could be gained. They both decided the paint, window curtains, and increased lighting would greatly add to a more cheerful imagery to anyone walking into the place.

The most difficult decision was what to name the place. It was now named *Main Street Café* though the only sign above the entry was a poorly blinking neon sign that simply said *Café*. David wondered if he ought to honor his grandfather by naming it "Harry's Café", but Laura vigorously voted him down, suggesting it be named "David's Place" instead. After days of bantering ideas back and forth, they both agreed that *"David's*

All-American Restaurant" would go a long way in convincing people coming from far and wide to take a moment and step inside a most inviting place to eat.

As far as deciding on a new menu, it came easy enough to decide what food Americans enjoyed eating, and Laura was a big help. Soda Fountain drinks would be a staple and the latest in cherry colas, lime-and lemon-flavored colas, root beer and cherry-flavored lemonade teas would be a must. The diner already had larger boilers behind the counter for making coffee and hot water for tea. David had hired a cook and one waitress from a Los Angeles café that he frequented when he and Laura and their friends would go bowling. It was a tiny place inside the bowling alley, and his food was always good, specializing in several kinds of burgers, always fresh and hot. It was easy enough to convince the two to move north with promises of a roomier kitchen, roomier dining room, and more salary. It was the roomier kitchen that convinced the cook named Sam to accept the job.

Sitting down together, the cook, the waitress, (his wife Marjorie) David and Laura created a new dinner menu of chicken and dumplings, pork chops, liver and onions, steak, beef stew and two kinds of homemade soups. Luncheon menus would offer four kinds of burgers, beef and turkey and tuna sandwiches, served with chips, pickles and a fresh coleslaw. Breakfast would probably remain much the same: eggs anyway you wanted, toast, hash browns, waffles, pancakes, hot oatmeal or cold cereals. Desserts were a puzzlement. The cook's wife, Marjorie, offered to make her grandmother's red-velvet cake recipe, an old southern recipe made with a cream cheese icing that she vowed was to die for. The cook had learned to make a decent bread pudding while a cook in the US Navy. David agreed, but wanting to add homemade pies, which no one came forward with because no one had confidence in making pies.

Having learned something as a houseboy at the Home of Ramona, Father decided to experiment at home with pie crusts and simple fillings. Mother found magazine recipes and helped him in their kitchen. Late one night around one o'clock, they both sat down to eat Father's fifth try at an apple pie. The crust was magnificent, crisp and flaky, holding up wonderfully to the hot, juicy sweetness of the apple filling. The filling held together nicely and did not run out of the pie, yet it fell away easily as the fork bit into it. Feeling greatly satisfied, and now confident in pie crust making, a scrumptious, homemade apple pie and cherry pie was added to their bill of fare.

The two weeks before their Grand Opening was a blur of activity. They did not see Harry, though Harry had delivered used furniture to their house over the last week. A large bed with two matching chests of drawers, a vanity set with a round etched glass mirror and a fabric round stool, a small green floral sofa and two matching chairs and one ottoman, end tables, lamps, area rugs, a formal dining room set with six chairs with a matching buffet, and of all things, an upright piano which no one knew how to play, were all delivered by truck from a local furniture dealer who accompanied the truck in his own car. He knocked at their door, as the back of the truck was opened, revealing the pile of proffered treasure. He showed David and Laura the paperwork and assured them both that Harry (who was well-known throughout the town) had paid cash for all this and instructed delivery at once. It was like Christmas day, Laura thought. She busied herself immediately instructing where the moving crew could place her new possessions. David called his grandfather " " to thank him while reporting their progress on the new café. It would open in eight days.

Sam and Marjorie helped my parents clean, scrub, sweep and paint from ceiling to floor and everything in between. They came early and went home late, their bodies wrapped in sore muscles. But each new morning they stood and assessed with a smile all that was being created. By the second to the last day, a new pillar and marquee neon sign was delivered and hung in place over the entry door. In bright orange and blue neon, the gas tubing spelling out "David's All-American Diner" fired up in full resonance. A sprinkle of stars in each corner made from white neon tubing added a singular but magical touch.

The sign was supposed to be Red, White and Blue, but the sign maker said the dark orange color was as close as he could get too red with the gases and material available to him so soon after the end of the war. He promised to improve on the color at the first opportunity he could.

As the four of them stood watching the sign all fired up, they were satisfied. The new sign, the lights shining from inside through dazzling clean and clear windows demonstrating new curtains, the lighted corner restaurant shined like a crystal clear lamp. It was powerfully satisfying for all of them as they gazed at the result of their collective energies.

Laura interviewed eight young girls, all recent graduates from the local high school, and she hired two of the more energetic and talkative ones for her new waitresses. They were both attractive and would please the customers. Marjorie was experienced and would handle the ten-stool counter. The two younger girls would wait on tables. She decided to run the cash register and fill in for the girls while on their breaks. David would meet and greet all the incoming guests and show them to their tables.

Harry was their eighteenth new customer. David greeted him, moving him to a seat at the counter because all ten booths were filled. Laura nodded as she busied herself with making change, and David pushed a large steak dinner in front of him, as Marjorie filled his coffee cup. It did not take Harry but ten minutes to eye the restaurant, it's new and cheery image, the booths filled with happy eating customers, and the jukebox blaring with a Big Band tune for him to realize just how successful, on his very first day, this restaurant would be. He was very pleased with what his grandson had accomplished. It made what he had to do even harder, but he refused to reflect on that. For now, he praised his grandson, patting him on the back and raising his glass of water in a cheerful, congratulatory manner.

Laura was grateful the cash register was crowded as she stole peeks at her husband and his grandfather. If she had not been busy David might have signaled for her to come greet him, and she did not wish to. She was afraid of this man, and despite all their success as a result of him, she did not relish having him in their lives, much less owing him such a great debt of not just money, but of gratitude. Such indebtedness left her feeling oddly cold and frightened.

It was a grueling yet happy two weeks. It was the end of January 1946, and rainy weather kept the customers pouring in if only to get out of the rain. But everyone, especially the local townsfolk, praised the cook as being far superior to the last owner. Mother had the bright idea of putting a guest book in front of the cash register so she could invite customers to write in their glowing compliments which she delighted to read to David every night. Each evening before they retired, weary and worn out, they made three apple pies and three cherry pies before crawling into bed.

Laura awoke the morning of February 7th expecting another day of their routine, when she threw back her bedding revealing and feeling a wetness and stickiness between her legs. Too new to motherhood to understand immediately what was happening, she sat and stared at herself and wondered if she was dying. When she awoke to the possibility her baby was in jeopardy, she screamed and then shouted for David.

He came running out of the bathroom with shaving cream on half his face, his eyes widening at the pool of wetness below her belly.

Neither thought of the natural cause and effect of a pregnant woman's water breaking. Both had assumed that this was indicative of impending dying and possible death. He used the chenille bedspread to wipe his chin, as he sped to her side, picking up her bathrobe on his way to her. "We have to get to the Emergency Room. Can you walk?" He asked her. "I- I think so," she responded nearly in tears. "Oh, David, I think I'm miscarrying. I think our baby is dying!"

Mumbling solicitous sentiments, David walked her in a careful, but swift manner to their car, placing her gently inside. Throwing only his jacket over his undershirt, he fished for his keys in his pants pocket and came around the driver's side of the car. The hospital was at the west end of town, and was literally ten minutes away.

Mother had taken the card Harry gave to David, indicating a Chinese Family Practitioner of medicine by the name of Doctor Eugene E. Dong. Suspicious, but realizing it was being paid for, Laura visited Dr. Dong in his small office at the back of his large white colonial house at the north end of town. Mother was delighted to hear he spoke perfect English with no discernible accent and after introductions, discovered he was an A-B-C

(American-born Chinese) raised by two Christian missionaries who brought back his abandoned and much pregnant fifteen-year-old mother to the United States. He was born in San Francisco's General Hospital and having every advantage his rich mentors could buy him and his mother, he went on to the best of schools, graduating with honors from Stanford University. He was a solemn but forthright doctor who employed a tolerant and cheerful Caucasian nurse. He was in his mid-fifties and had recently moved from San Francisco to the sleepy community of Salinas four years ago to get away from the corruption of city life. He wanted to treat and heal people instead of battling the egregious ignorance of crime, vice and bigotry that filled big cities. He had a pleasant-looking Chinese wife whom he had met at Stanford. They had two sons, both living and working in San Francisco as attorneys exclusively working for the San Francisco and Oakland Chinatown's Tong Associations against the constant embattlements of City Hall and State persecution of Chinese. His Chinese wife, though not American-born, was an intelligent woman whose passion was writing about American injustices levied on her Asian brethren. She had made the FBI's "Watch-List" by the time she was nineteen, and Dong had discovered her as she was passing out anti-government literature on campus. It was only by the grace of his medical practice that the FBI was kept at bay, even though agents came to question their recent move to Monterey County.

    Dr. Dong was more compassionate and understanding, having lived both as an American, as well as preserving his Chinese culture. He tolerated the high and mighty attitudes of his colleagues who never viewed him as an equal, because he often knew more than they did, and with his quiet, unobtrusive knowledge, he rarely misdiagnosed, often healed and provided greater medical care and treatment than did his haughty counterparts. Generally, his successes in life, after a while, shut the mouths of those egotists who thought themselves superior to him. But here ensconced in a lovely white and sprawling house, nestled among vineyards and pumpkin patches, Dr. Dong, came to know inner peace and contentment as a small practice doctor in Salinas, California.

Laura and David Fong's personal story was fascinating to him. He anxiously re-told the story to his wife the evening after he first met Laura Fong. A white woman fell in love, and married a Chinese man in this day and age. He found that miraculous. His less approving wife found it abominable. "Utter foolishness," she flatly told him.

But on this day, Eugene Dong answered his ringing telephone and was told by an unnamed hospital nurse that Laura Fong was being admitted. He was needed to oversee the birth of her first baby.

Mother gave birth to her first child, a baby girl, on February 7, 1946 at ten minutes until two in the afternoon. There was no family, no other loved ones, except her husband by her side. Somehow, holding her new baby, she suddenly did not feel as alone as she once had been. She had just made a new family of her own.

In the ensuing months, their restaurant business grew as fast as their new baby. Mother gave over her cash register duties to Marjorie, and the waitresses shifted by taking on more duties to cover for Mother's absence as she and her new baby got acquainted.

Generally, young girls who have their first child have their mothers, their grandmothers, their aunts and friends to help coach them what to expect with a newborn. Mom had no one but Doctor Dong to coach her, and he made himself available to her phone calls any time of the night or day. She had many questions and many frustrations with her first baby.

Father worked long and hard making the restaurant a success, and by the increase in the crowds, and the appreciation of the jukebox music with the local youth, it was difficult to find empty seats, especially Friday and Saturday nights.

Though both were exhausted, the feeling of their exhaustion had a foundation of success. It all felt good. For the first time, they were succeeding in every aspect of their mortal lives together. They had a place they could call home. They had a successful business, and a new baby gave them the satisfaction of being a real Family. Their hearts expanded, and the pressures of finding acceptance in this world designed to ignore or persecute them backed far away from them at last. Though their neighbors stayed away from the house on Archer Street where a White woman and her baby lived with an Asian man, they found enough to give them happiness on a level both found accommodating.

The one thorn was Grandpa Harry. Mother's sense of security, her sense of well-being and happiness depended upon seeing as little of Grandpa Harry as possible. She left those meetings for David to handle, and indeed, when Harry came to visit, he usually came to the restaurant during business hours and Mother was rarely there. Each encounter reminded Mother that her happy little world was based on Harry giving them everything, and them owing him beyond what they could not possibly pay back. Each time she saw him, his eyes would often fix on her as though he was shutting out the entire world and concentrating his gaze just upon her. It was a cold stare. It was an evil stare. David, of course, never noticed and told her she exaggerated, but Mother knew Harry did not approve of her.

Harry did, however, approve of the baby even though she turned out to be a girl and not the requisite boy child. He cooed and clucked and made silly faces in her face. Mother wanted to laugh and wished she had a camera to capture his silly dancing and prancing around her baby so that he could elicit a baby smile or a baby laugh. On the thirtieth day, or the first month birthday of their baby, he gave a solid gold necklace, with a solid gold pendant, and a solid gold ring to match, along with a baby-wrist sized jade bracelet. He told Laura that Chinese babies celebrated their first 30 days of life with gold and jade representing health and prosperity. Mother politely thanked him and silently felt the gifts useless for a baby and ostentatious even for an adult. Mother had never even seen 24 karat gold anything and wondered where he bought these items.

The happier times were when Harry stayed away or was not seen or heard from. The restaurant business provided Harry with his thirty percent on a very regular basis, and therefore, Harry had little excuse to call or visit them, though he came often enough to the restaurant to visit and ask after his grandbaby.

The routines of their days and nights played out without incident, and everyone seemed happy in their pursuits. They had developed many friendships with those locals who frequented their restaurant, and Mother felt those friendships were nice, but superficial. She supposed that most did not know and could not assume that she was married to the Chinese man who owned the restaurant they were so happy with. Her cadre of waitresses was instructed not to say anything, and because they liked Mom and Dad, as well as their jobs, they did as they were instructed. It made fitting in to their community that much easier. Both Mom and Dad learned to play down their marriage to avoid the awkward explanations. Public signs of affection were no longer allowed or invited. Their baby was another matter. She looked Asian. On many occasions, Mother was asked if she was babysitting another woman's child. Even when she offered an explanation, "No, this is my baby," most people assumed she must have adopted a foreign baby. As far as Mother was concerned, she felt few people deserved a lengthy and truthful explanation. She simply did not wish to invite their bigotry. So, life went on.

It was Halloween, the end of October 1946 and Mother was home preparing a home-cooked meal, which she rarely made. On most occasions, they both ate leftover chicken or pot roast brought home from the restaurant. She had shopped all day, buying food, dessert and a special little gift for David. She also had wrapped candies that she gave out to the neighborhood trick or treaters earlier in the evening before she knew David would be home. It was midnight when he finally came in and the look on his face gave her concern.

"What's wrong? Why are you so late?" she asked as she met him at the door. He noticed the lit candles on the dining room table, the lace tablecloth, and their best dishes set out. He had missed an occasion, it seemed.

"I have some good news, and some bad news," was his reply. "What did I miss here?"

"Oh, don't worry about that. I'll explain after I hear your news," she answered.

He took off his coat, laid it on the hook by the entry door, and walked past her to the dining room. He picked up the small box so beautifully wrapped with a green ribbon that he hesitated with his news. "Maybe I ought to hear your news," he said, "I think it might be better than mine."

"David," was all she said in a tone that made him understand he'd better quit stalling and tell her before she did him harm.

"Sit down, and I'll tell you my day," he moved his arm to the small of her back and steered her toward their small settee. Sitting knee to knee, facing each other, hands in each other's hands, he began.

"You remember that I told you I was sold as a baby. That I never knew my real parents, but that I remember having two sisters." At this, mother nodded, making affirmative sounds, urging him to continue.

"My Ni-Ni, that mean old lady who bought me, well, she's sick. She may be dying. We don't know, but Grandpa has asked me to go back to her village. She needs help and modern medicine, and she's willing to tell me who my real parents are. She says they will be waiting when I arrive." His voice was shaky, but excited. She could see in his eyes a kind of pleading that wasn't in his voice.

She looked him in his eyes, and asked, "When will you leave?"

"Grandfather has a ticket for a flight to San Francisco this coming Friday. The boat to China leaves Saturday morning." he told her, but his eyes looked down to his hands. He could feel her anxiety anticipated by the squeeze of her fingers in his hands.

"How long will you be gone," she asked searching for his eyes again?

"Two, maybe four months," came his slow response. At this, their hands flew apart as Laura Mae leapt from the sofa, and fairly ran to the dining room.

"Laura, Honey! I'll get to find out who my real family is! What my real name was! I don't want to leave you, but I can't miss this opportunity!" He was at her side in an instant, grabbing her shoulders from behind to steady her, to steady him, as he continued.

"'I have made arrangements already for the restaurant to run itself while I'm gone. You won't have to do anything, or even go there unless you want to visit. They will be fine and Grandpa promised he will watch over you and the baby and ensure you get anything you need," he told her.

At the mention of Harry, Laura stiffened, and then her shoulders sagged. She could not say no. She knew from all their intimate conversations this was too important to him and with all their newfound happiness, finding his real family would begin a new happy chapter for them both. Perhaps it meant a loving family who would embrace them instead of rejecting them as she felt with Harry. Perhaps it would mean Harry, his sons, and that horrid grandmother might all fade away from their lives with the coming forth of his own real family. The thought of replacing Harry provided a sudden positive boost to the negative of David's leaving for so long. What would she do for four months without her husband?

David whispered in her ear, "What was your news?"

In silent response, Laura picked up the little box with the green ribbon, and handed it to him, as she blew out the ebbing candle tapers. "Open it," she instructed him. While she gave him his task, she was calculating the months he would be absent, and whether or not she could do this all alone.

David pulled the ribbon, pulled the box lid off, and sorted the tissue paper. He pulled out and held up a baby's single little booty and lifted one eyebrow. He stared for a few seconds at the booty, and then his eyes queried her as it dangled between their heads.

"We're having another baby," she answered his silent query.

Chapter 19

David's mouth felt dry, and his head pounded as he walked up the gangplank of the USS Roosevelt. Harry had purchased his steerage and arranged for all his travel papers. He gave him a large trunk filled with things for his grandmother, including western medicines provided by Doctor Dong that Harry told him would help treat his wife's ailments. Harry told David that he might save the woman's life, and his mission of mercy was extremely important to the Family. He gave David explicit instructions, and the names of those who would be meeting him in Canton to take him into the interior. Father had no memory, and simply no idea of how to reach the village he lived in for such a short few years before he left. He had some memory of the old lady there, and some of his old friends who played with him or watched over him in the village. He remembered the ox that he and others would ride to school on. This time, there would be a car to transport him back to the village, driven by someone who knew how to get there. It would be a matter of hours, and not days to reach the village now.

He could not decide if he felt ill because he was leaving his pregnant wife alone for several months, or if the thought of seeing his Ni-Ni and China again, or even meeting his real Family was making his head throb and his stomach roil. He wondered if he would feel this queasy anxiety for the entire twenty-two days of his expected voyage. He even wondered if the excursion out to sea would compound his physical turmoil with seasickness.

He finally found his cabin, deep below, following the crew's directions. He hastily opened the cabin door, saw two small beds a chair, a small round table and a round mirror. He threw his suitcase on one bed, and threw his body onto the other, closing his eyes against the desire to throw up. He wanted very much to fall asleep, but only got about ten minutes into that singular effort when the cabin door crashed open, and in walked his cabin mate. David jumped up as though he had been caught at something unseemly. He grabbed for his suitcase on the other bed and offered an apology for messing both beds.

The man gave Dad a wide grin from a dark-skinned and large head. The head was made larger by an incredible abundance of exceptionally curly long hair. The man appeared to be a Polynesian.

"Is okay, brah!" the man said. "I take dis bunk, yeah?" He threw a canvas sack on the bed closest to the door. "Name Kimo, Brah. Me from Fiji, you know? Island Fiji, yeah?"

"I'm David. Nice to meet you." Dad replied as he sat his suitcase down and sat on the bed opposite.

"Where you go, Brah?" Kimo asked.

"I'm returning to my Village, the Yee Village East of Canton to see my family," my Father offered.

"Good, man," Kimo said, "I cook. I meet my ship the *Doreen* in Canton Harbor. I ship out for two years, then back to Frisco, yeah!"

When Dad said nothing, he added, "Is good life, sea cook. Lots fresh fish, Brah. Good eel, good squid." He laughed as David closed his eyes against his growing nausea. "You no look so good, Brah." Kimo gave Dad another big grin and a deep chuckle. "We ain't out to sea yet!" Kimo reached out and slapped

David's knee, and Dad gave him a weak grin in return. It promised to be a long voyage if he didn't get to feeling better. So, he excused himself and told Kimo he was going for a walk hoping the fresh air would clear his head and calm his stomach. Kimo shrugged and reached into his kit pulling out a comic book and a pint bottle of gin, and rolled on his bed as Dad closed the door.

The days seemed to fly by. David's stomach and head did clear and was replaced with the jovial and jocular companionship of his shipmate. Kimo Kahui Mounga was a most amiable and funny man. The laughter made all the difference in the long and protracted voyage. They played cards a great deal, all types of games learned in the Merchant Marines. He spoke of his sailing adventures, in what he referred to as "talk story". He came from a large Fijian family of eleven children and a drunk father who tried to be abusive, but the mother beat him up before he could raise a hand. "She one tough waihini," explained Kimo. "She beat all us!" Everything he said fascinated Dad, and he filed away a deep desire to visit the Islands Kimo spoke of so fondly. But it was his practical jokes that kept Father sleeping with one eye open.

  He was Kimo's first victim because he was so accessible. Finding it fitful to sleep his first night, Dad was in a deep state of sleep when he felt a tickling on his face. He swatted a bit, his head turning away from the offending touch. But waking to what he thought was a spider or flying insect, he slapped more vigorously at his face, felt a spongy splash of something wet which forced himself to wake up more fully. He saw his cabin mate rolling on the bed guffawing, holding his stomach, his face scrunched in laughter. Dad placed his head forward to see his reflection in the round mirror opposite his bed and found the side of his face covered in foam. He looked ridiculous. He smelled his hand also covered in foam remnants. It smelled of spice and soap. Shaving cream came to mind. No one had ever pulled such a trick on him, not in the Chinese community which raised him and he hesitated laughing with Kimo about it, he wasn't sure that was appropriate. Wasn't he supposed to be angry at this? Was he being laughed at? As he used his bed linen to wipe his head and his hand, he was becoming more awake and as he did the concept of laughter and a joke played on him while he slept became more appealing. He laughed and that made Kimo laugh harder. Kimo finally rose from his bed and offered a hand in wiping off the soap that he missed. Dad was glad this man would be his roommate and not another enemy.

Kimo found tremendous opportunities to show Father how to do mischief aboard their vessel. Like an apprentice, Kimo showed Dad every practical joke he could. Kimo had several packets of small Chinese firecrackers that popped more than they banged, but it was sufficient to make women scream and men jump. Water closets were strategically placed throughout the decks, giving passengers toilet conveniences on the outside of the ship. Each room had a small circular window that generally remained slightly open to refresh the air of each small compartment. Taking their morning walk, Kimo had Dad light each firecracker, and looking around them, quickly dropped the tiny paper stick of gun powder and moved on. A few seconds later, came the reward of a pop and the cries of his victims. Having made friends with the ship's cook, Kimo would always borrow a raw egg, placing the egg in the bowl of hard-boiled eggs set amongst the breakfast buffet. Taking seats that gave them the advantage of watching the diners, they would wait until their victim began to peel away the eggshell. It especially was funny when the unsuspecting slammed the egg down to break the shell and found themselves covered in raw egg.

Kimo's most disgusting trick was the dead bugs and animals. His bag held a shoebox, and inside was a variety of nasty rotting corpses. The box was filled with huge dead cockroaches, small, tiny snakes, squashed and flattened toads and frogs, flies, spiders and things that Father could not identify clearly; these were special prizes. Each day, he picked out a few choice candidates and placed them in his pocket. As they made their way to the dining hall, he would scope out women reading their books in deck chairs. Women were his favorite tease because they elicited high-toned, but effective screams. Men would jump away but rarely screamed. Women would scream, jump and took considerable time to calm down. Well worth the effort. They would spy a woman alone, reading a book or a magazine and one who had a table beside her, hopefully, with a drink on it. Waiting was part of the payoff and sometimes it took the better part of the day to unload the corpses. But in the end, the woman's attention was diverted with quick conversation and flattery while the bug was placed on the table or in her drink, and the moved quickly on to a vantage point where they could witness the scenario unfold from a safe distance. Sometimes the weight of the insect made it drop to the bottom of their cup or glass and would not be discovered until the glass was drained of liquid. The longer the wait, the more delicious the misdemeanor.

The amusements, the card games, the songs he sang accompanied by his small ukulele, the friendly talk helped to ease my father's anxiety, and as they neared their port in Canton, Dad wrote out his address to Kimo and gave it to him. "You are my first real friend, Kimo." my father declared. "I am grateful to have known you." He asked him to write when he could.

Having exchanged each other's stories at the beginning of the voyage, Kimo summed it up. "You find your real family, David. Bring 'em home. Aloha, Brah!" He grabbed my father's small frame and enveloped it into his large arms, squeezing him to his round belly. They would repeat this goodbye at the end of the gangplank the very next day as they parted company.

After saying goodbye to Kimo, Father's attentions turned swiftly to the task before him. He searched the crowded pier for someone looking for him. After three or four passes through the throngs, his eyes rested upon a small man dressed in black pants, a white undershirt, and black thongs. He looked like a country villager, a coolie among the jumble of merchants, tourists and obvious missionaries dressed in western clothing. The villager was holding a sign written in Chinese characters in front of him. This would be difficult, but he thought it read "YEE". As he approached the man, he asked "Are you looking for Kwok Hing Yee?" he asked in Cantonese. "Are you from the Yee Village?"

The man kowtowed in front of him, softly replying that he was sent to pick up Kwok Hing Yee and bring him back to his grandmother. The sign had worked at clearing up that matter. He was surprised at the use of his adopted name which he had not used since immigrating to the United States. Yet it made sense, because this was the name given to him by his Ni-Ni. How else would she recall him, except by the name bestowed him after she purchased him. He decided not to tell her his new name was now David Lee Fong. Even though it was a paper-son name, he preferred it because it distanced him from the dreaded Yee Family. Knowing he was going back to the nest of origin; he felt his old resentments rising up from the pit of his stomach. The woman who took him from his real family would be waiting for him. Will she willingly give him back to his real family? Would they also be there waiting for his return? With no memory of them, would he find love for them? Would they still love him, or did they sell him to be well rid of him? The journey was just beginning.

Chapter 20

The journey took twenty-six hours with several breaks to stretch, eat, relieve their bladders and fuel the car with water and petrol. David found the remarkable changes to this once dirt road and the little townships and enterprises that grew up along the road to be remarkable, though he had little memory of it. He simply remembered that the houses, the fuel stations, the food stands were all new, and these new enterprises brought more people to the once empty road and widened the road considerably. It was still a dirt road but improved and nearly commercially graded for the convenience of automobiles and trucks. The former wagon ruts were now gone.

Even so, as they approached the outer lands, heading for the distant Himalayan mountains, commerce fell away, and their journey toward the Yee Village ended in solitary and empty landscape. The road narrowed at the foothills of the last mountain and it split both to the right and left. The driver continued forward on the center road and in about thirty minutes crested the top of the mountain. As the front of the vehicle fell into a downward cast from the summit, a beautiful valley opened, and at last, familiarity and memory came together in Father's head. He knew before asking that they approached the Yee Village at last. He wiped his face with his handkerchief and began to self-consciously adjust his clothing.

The car pulled up in front of the old Teak house. The plants were taller around the house but little else had changed the façade from what he remembered. The mother-of-pearl inlay in the teak doors were faded from the colors they once held, but they remained intricate in their workmanship.

An old woman dressed in black came out and kowtowed. Was this one of the young girl servants now grown older? He could not remember her name. She motioned for him to enter. As he did, he came into an empty room. No family greeted him. The old woman in black left him standing alone, disappearing around the rice paper divider. As he toured the room with his eyes and fingered the small figurines around the edges of the room, he heard voices, one in particular barking orders to the other softer voices. Perhaps his Ni-Ni was so ill, she could not leave her bed.

But in another few minutes, three people entered the room and stood waiting before him. Supported by the one old woman and another younger girl, David's eyes rested upon the central figure being held up by the other two. The shriveled and shrunken old woman whom he used to fear and who made others quake and tremble stood frailly before him, teetering between the two struggling servants. She smiled, and held out her arms. He answered her signal and approached her with a kiss to the cheek and a soft greeting in Chinese. He took her out of the arms of her servants and gently escorted her to a well-padded high-backed chair and took a short stool sitting well below her arm. Another servant entered with a tray of tea and dim sum. In time, her hand came to rest on top of his head. He put down his tea and looked up at her.

"I have dreamt of this day," she said. "How many times have I dreamt of the triumphal return of my new son? My 'second chance' son!"

Not knowing how to reply, my father said, "We heard you were ill, Grandmother. If so, I have brought western medicines to help restore you and many other fine gifts from America…"

"Bah! What need have I of western pills and concoctions? Our medicine goes back centuries before the white devils' medicine. You bring me nothing I want nor need, except you! You are more precious a gift than even gold. I have waited for you a very, very long time. YOU are the reason I am still alive. Your return has been my medicine."

Indeed, she even looked less fragile than when she first appeared, as though she gathered strength from his nearness.

The conversation dropped off into a chasm of awkwardness which he struggled to get out of. Finally, gathering his thoughts, Father spoke, "Grandfather and your sons send you their love and concern. They continue to labor and work hard to be successful in their work. Grandfather has set me up with my own restaurant in Salinas…uh, that's in California, below San Francisco."

"I know of my husband and of my other sons. I have their reports. I know of their businesses. It may be strange to you that we communicate from two different worlds, but they have been very good to report their lives to me," she interrupted him. "They have even told me about your marriage to a *fan quay*, a white ghost." Her gaze became intense, passion fueled with a challenge crossing her face.

"My wife is a beautiful woman. Yes, she is not Chinese, but I have fallen in love with her world and her beauty. We have a baby girl, and another child is expected in…"

It surprised him how quickly she cut off his words.

For such an elderly woman, there was no degradation of her speech or the words she used. "Let us not discuss your American family right at this moment. You are here, now, with me in China, your birthplace, your home. You are home now. I have pictured this day for many, many years. Do not rob me of my revelry."

She continued, "You must be tired. We have prepared for you a small feast to celebrate your homecoming. The villagers have prepared some dancing and some singing for your homecoming. It is a big occasion for us all, and then we want to see what you have brought back from the Gold Mountain in that big trunk of yours."

She instructed one of her servants to show him his room at the opposite side of the house from her rooms where he could wash up and change into cooler, lighter clothing for dinner. No electricity existed in this remote village, despite its widespread use in most cities in China. It amazed my father still in the age of modern plumbing, that here in this back country, they still used huge hand-carved bowls to pour pitchers of water for bathing. Large bathing was still done with servants attending, and David did not wish strange hands to attend him. Elimination was still done in one of two ornate wooden shacks to the rear of the house. In the ancient custom of the Chinese, farmers still used human waste to fertilize some of their fields. Father hoped his years away from this home-grown food would not make him sick. His childhood here already gave him a lifetime of malaria, and a bout with scarlet fever left him with an enlarged heart.

He freshened up with cool water and a sweet-smelling hand-milled soap, changed into a loose white shirt and a pair of cotton shorts. He took a wet cloth with him to hang around his neck, so dense was the heat and humidity.

Finding his grandmother outdoors on the veranda, a long table was set before him, candles and torches had been lit in the ebb of the early evening, as the sun hung like an orange ball just above the mountains. It would set on the other side of those mountains in a matter of minutes. For now, the orange hue of the setting sun blended with the purple haze of the well heated but diminishing sky. The green reflection of her rice paddies, and vegetable fields and the brown of her thatched houses and wooden fences and animal pens created a beautiful and serene landscape for him to take in. He paused and observed all his eyes could take in, his hands, on the teak railing of her veranda. The buzz of insects was as a faint roar of wilderness.

"Shall I meet my real parents tonight, Ni-Ni?" He asked her without looking at her.

"They could not come tonight, my son. They no longer live nearby. Your real mother and father left our nearby village to move back to the Canton. They both work at city jobs now and must travel later when they can arrange to leave their city jobs. I do not understand it all myself, but they will write to tell us when they can come," came her matter-of-fact reply.

He turned to face her. She was just finishing washing her hands in a bowl of rose-petal water held up by the old servant and reached for a towel to dry her fingers.

"What about my two sisters? I remember my sisters."

"Yes. Good! You have a good memory. Yes, two twin girls five years older than you. You will be pleased to know they are both married, both have children," she told him. "Unfortunately, I never kept track of the girls after they married, so I am uninformed as to their whereabouts. I expect your parents will tell you the details. We shall ask them to bring, oh, what they call those paper images... oh! Yes, photographs!" She mispronounced the word, "photographs" poorly, as though the word was from a foreign language. She gestured to David.

"Come. Sit here, next to me. I am informed our feast is ready, and see, the sun sets and our stage begins."

David sat down and as he did, she motioned with her hand, and music from a gallery of players sitting below her veranda began to play. Servers from both the left and right of the veranda brought forward bowl after bowl of foods, fruits and drink. Soon, others sat at the table, important guests, the head caretaker or mayor of the Yee Village, his wife and son, a Chinese Fortune Teller, and his wife, a Buddhist priest, and Daoist teacher from the school he used to attend. Introductions were made, the food laid down and after conversations and eating died down, dancers and stories were played out in front of the house steps before the guests.

Father had a difficult time following the conversations at first. After a twenty-year absence, his Chinese was a bit rusty. By the end of the evening, however, it was easier to understand, as his ears became more accustomed in translating what he heard into English in his head. They had many questions about America for him and he was grateful to answer them. He felt their most basic fears and misunderstandings of all things American came out in their strange questions. But no one asked about his wife.

"Is it true Brother?" asked the Buddhist priest, "that Americans all carry guns and teach their young to kill and hunt their prey?"

"I was told American white woman sleep with many male partners and use chemicals to bleach their skin and hair. Is this true?" asked the caretaker's wife who softly giggled with embarrassment behind her hands.

"The White Devils worship gold and dress carelessly with too many layers and cover their heads and hands with vanity and jewels. They are wasteful with their money and are fat and lazy," commented the Fortune Teller. His wife smiled as she looked down at her unadorned hands. Father was greatly amused at their unfounded concepts, and tried his best to clarify and correct, though he took their blanks stares and tittering laughter at what he told them a sign of unbelief.

The meal was delicious, and thankfully, except for the lights from the candles and torches, he could not see the ingredients very well to tell what he had eaten. This was not the Chinese food he had in America. He was grateful that he packed some American medicines to help with any digestive problems he might encounter. He brought purifying tablets to drink the water and made sure his tea was properly boiled before serving.

The meal ended. The dancers and storytellers finished their program. David, grateful for something to do, opened the trunk that sat in a corner and began the grand presentation.

Several bolts of cloth were presented, including satins, cottons, and light wools. Lace, buttons, and threads were also produced. Dried spices, and canned goods appeared with explanation and a pearl necklace was given in a flourish of "oohs" and "ahhs". David presented each guest with small travel postcards of American landmarks: The Golden Gate Bridge, Mount Rushmore, the Whitehouse, New York's iconic Empire State building, a field of tulips, a rose garden in Pasadena, City Hall in Los Angeles, a view of the Pacific Coastline and Yosemite National Park. These pictures were enjoyed immensely, and passed quickly from one to another and round again. The medicines were displayed with an explanation of what they did, but the names were most curious because they did not seem to recognize the names of any herbs.

Finally, a toast was made to his Ni-Ni and to David, welcoming him home, and giving gratitude for their feast, and the guests went home. Servants appeared to lift his grandmother up from her seat, as she bid him goodnight.

"Ah! A fine feast! A good meal! A great occasion. Sleep, now, my son. Time enough for what we have to do," she told him.

"What was it we have to do," he wondered to himself. He hesitated, but then reached over to kiss her cheek. He watched her as her two servants turned her around and slowly disappeared into the house with her in the middle. He sat on the veranda steps as the rest of the household carried away plates, bowls and food, whisking it all away rather quickly. He enjoyed two cigarettes, thinking of his wife and daughter, before turning toward his own room and the bed surrounded by netting that awaited him.

David learned that the serenity of the evening would be significantly different in the early morning hours. By dawn, he awoke to voices, yelling, calling and communicating with a loudness that defeated the buzzing of the insects. He looked at the netting surrounding his short bed and saw that he was grateful for its protection during the night. Several large beetles and winged creatures had entangled themselves in the netting, and he kicked at them with his bare feet. A female servant appeared with a tray of tea and dumplings, and another came close behind her with a broom made of twined sticks which she now used to brush away the accumulation of bugs from the netting and the floor around him. They smiled and bowed before him as they went about their tasks. When he asked if his Ni-Ni was up yet, they smiled, kowtowed and backed out of his room. He rose, washed a bit, and dressed for the day. He came out to find many people washing down the tables used the night before for their banquet. The floors of the veranda were being scrubbed and re-oiled. The lanterns were being dismantled. He was amazed at the number of people who set about taking down and cleaning. This village held a lot of people, he thought.

He brought his tea and dumplings with him and sat down to light a cigarette. He still felt strange, as though he was suddenly cast in a film now being shot in rural China. He wanted someone to give him directions on how to act, what to say, what to do and where to stand. His direction came from behind him, as his Ni-Ni came into view.

"You smoke too much, my son," she observed. "It hardens your lungs and draws longevity from your chi."

"You are probably right," he replied. "It is a very bad habit that most Americans enjoy."

"Then you had best give up these American habits that tempt to draw away your life," she said without looking at him. Silence leapt from the last of her words, as he watched her lift her head and sniff the air. She seemed to look past the labors of those working around her as though they did nothing important to her. At last, she spoke, still not looking directly at him.

"I have a task for you, that is very important to this village. Will you accept such a challenge?" She asked.

"I am willing to help you with any task while I am here, Ni-Ni," came his swift reply.

You are Number One Son while you are here. The whole of all our villages knows this. In the Cheung Village that neighbors ours, they require a new well to be dug. They have the tools and the manpower, but there is no overlord to see this task is done properly, and in time. The Village needs the water, and we cannot continue to send them barrels of our own. Do you remember how far they are?" she asked him, staring straight ahead.

"" It is where I went to school, riding Tak-Tak, that old water buffalo." His face brightened into a smile of remembrance. "It's not far."

"Nevertheless, you are too old to ride on the back of a filthy beast. I have a truck now that will take you and bring you home. Supervise their work, make sure the well is deep enough and plentiful for living. Make them work well and long to get the work done." His Ni-Ni's face was set in the stern but cool fashion he remembered. Her eyelids drooped over her pupils, dispelling any doubt to her ruling hand. This was not a woman who entertained disappointment.

"I will be happy to take on this task for you and the Villagers." David stood and tried to bow to her as he left to return to his room to change into work clothes. He came back a few minutes later in a white T-shirt and dungarees. The sight of his clothing caused the old woman to gasp and expel a Chinese oath under her breath. He put on a pair of round green pilot sunglasses, and seeing the truck waiting for him on the road below her house, he said a swift good-bye and ran down the hill to meet it.

Happy to have something to do, David jumped into the truck cab and slammed the door. The driver who came in after him was a tall boy. He could not have been more than fifteen years of age. It made David feel odd, but he was beginning to accept the unexpected knowing he was in a "foreign" land.

When he asked in careful Chinese, the boy answered in English that he was thirteen, adding a "sir" at the end of his response. It surprised him, and he broke into a wide smile. "Where did you learn to speak English?" David asked.

"We have missionary in school now, we stay after school and learn American, speak American good. I go Gold Mountain someday, too. I be like Clark Gable movie," he grinned. The entire ride, the boy asked question after question about Hollywood and movie stars. The boy had seen one Clark Gable film in Canton two years ago when he drove to the City for Village supplies. It was the first film he had ever seen.

In roughly five miles, they came across a small village, surrounded with a low mud and brick wall with bamboo trellis' atop the wall structure, through which bushes bearing bright red flowers flourished. When they turned into the gate, what appeared to be the entire village was lining the narrow street and shouts and waves greeted them as they drove along. The boy smiled and honked the truck horn noisily, making the villagers volume of cheers increase. David felt like he was in a parade, or being received home as a hero might. He felt a bit embarrassed and confused over the fuss people made.

At last, after a few meandering turns through the small village of stone and mud mortar, they arrived at the back of the village, and soon came upon the work site for the new well. Several muddied workers were pulling on a rope through a pulley system centered over a large gaping hole in the ground, supported by a series of neatly and tightly tied bamboo poles. The pulley conveyed a large wicker basket being lowered into and out of the big hole. Below boys loaded the basket with scoops of mud. The men above heaved the large load of mud, while others grabbed the basket and emptied it into a mound being reduced by other workers with wooden shovels.

David exited the truck, and all the workers came to a halt. The boy who drove the truck announced to everyone present that The Firstborn had returned to dictate their work and oversee their success for the entire Village. Again, David felt embarrassed, especially when they all began to kowtow in front of him.

He made his way carefully to the hole, surveyed it, as they watched in approving silence. The hole was approximately ten feet deep, and about eight feet wide. Four small young boys were down at the bottom, attached to ropes, scooping mud with large bowls. They looked up and hailed him, their dirty faces being wiped with dirty hands. He saw mostly happy eyes and teeth smiling out of muddy faces. The floor of the hole was damp, but they were not standing in water yet, which meant they 'had not reached a water table. They explained that the ropes were tied to each boy so if water or mud flowed unexpectedly into the hole, the men above could pull the boys out quickly. It was difficult to follow what each was saying, as they talked over each other in excitement, wanting to impress the "First-born" with their well-making wisdom. The boy who drove him stepped in to interpret his broken English.

"When boys finish, men go down to mud walls, set stone and mortar, let all dry before digging more," the boy told him. "They glad you here. Say you bring luck. No one drown. No one hurt on this job with you here."

"I hope to God that's true," he said in English to the boy. "Stick close to me boy, I need you to interpret what they are saying. My Chinese, not so good." They both laughed.

A week of hard work had passed, and David felt good about his "supervision." In truth, they taught him a great deal about setting stone, mixing mortar, and well design. This well was a "dry" well, and further up the village hillside, other men were digging for a water table, while still others worked at cutting, burning and fitting bamboo pipe taken from the surrounding mountain groves, to use as conduits for the water. Trenches were dug out and bamboo pipe was laid toward the dry well. A bamboo spout would be inserted near the bottom of the first well, and when all the stone was placed and the well cleaned out and dry ready for storage, the other pipe would be connected to well spring, and the bamboo line would fill with rushing spring water and be compelled by the pipe to run toward the first well. David did not understand how they could locate a well spring without a hydroelectric engineer, but he quickly reminded himself that China was older than any country on the face of the earth, making their ancient practices greater than modern-day science.

He enjoyed the hands-on training and breaking for lunch brought by the wives and children of the workers. It was gratifying and happy work, and his companions found David and his westernization fascinating and attractive. There was much talk and much laughter. He would come home at the end of the day covered in mud, a smile on his face. After showering in an outdoor area behind the main house, he dressed in cool silk pajamas, enjoyed a light supper, drank his tea and smoked his cigarettes as he watched the twinkling of lights from the torches across the village. He never saw the Old Woman at night, and assumed she retired hours ago. He had to tell her that he would need to leave as soon as the well was finished. He somehow knew he would probably never see his real parents as he had originally hoped. Perhaps before he left, she would give information about what city they now lived in so that he could see them before he left China altogether. Or perhaps she could give him their names and an address where he could write them a letter. It would solve everything inside him.

Now that he was sure the old woman was not (yet) dying, he was more than anxious to get home to his wife and Family, but he had made this promise to help with this well and would finish it before leaving.

Almost another week passed before he saw the Old Woman again. She was sitting on the large veranda, the setting sun bathing her face in its orange and misty glow, as he approached the house. "You look as though you played with the pigs," she said. "Go! Wash yourself, and then come sit with me."

He nodded silently as he went around to the back of the house. He returned, fresh, damp and cooler in a white set of silk pajamas and slippers. Her servants always left soap, towels and fresh clean clothing for him at the shower room each and every day. It was, he thought, very pampering.

Dinner and tea were already waiting for him. After a few bites, he settled into his chair, and turned toward the Old Woman. "Ni-Ni," he broached. "The well will be completed by Saturday, and the Villagers are preparing a feast to celebrate the occasion. Now that I have accomplished the task you gave me, and now that I know you are not ill, I must return to my wife and Family." He lit a cigarette and wondered why his hands trembled as he did.

There was a small moment of silence before she responded. She continued to gaze out over her village, not looking directly at him, as she finally spoke. "What wife? What family do you speak of? You have no wife. You have no family but me."

Stunned, David stood up so quickly it was as though her words burned him. "Grandmother, I have a wife in California. She bears me children. I must return!"

"SIT DOWN!" she yelled at him. "You are never to stand over me and tell me what you must do! I will tell YOU." David sat down hard into his chair.

Seeing his obedience, she continued: "That White Devil that bears you babies is not your true wife and cannot be. She is, your concubine, your whore…"

"Grandmother, please…" Father pleaded.

"Do NOT interrupt! She shouted with a force that demanded his silence. His heart was pounding. "The White Woman cannot be your true wife. You have returned to your Village to have a proper Chinese wedding to a proper Chinese wife. This has been our plan and it has been decided."

"Decided by *who*?" David asked angrily.

"Your Grandfather has corresponded with me for some months over this matter. He sent you home for this purpose and I approve. You will properly wed, and you will stay here in China with me. Then when I die, you will be Lord over all our properties.

A small silence again. David began slowly, his head swimming with too much deception, lies, and fear.

"I am already a legally married man. I love my wife and I need to go home *now*," he calmly emphasized with a low, firm voice. He noted his fists were tightly closed as he tried to maintain his calm.

"You are in China," she said turning to face him for the first time. The set of her face set his heart pounding quicker. She spoke slowly, "We do not recognize your laws, or your marriage to a white woman. Your grandfather tells me that even your own people and hers 'do not recognize your so-called marriage. You think you have not brought shame and anger upon your Chinese Family? We, *boy*, are the only people who are your people! Your white woman is nothing to us. You will never, *ever* see her again!"

"I don't have to listen to this! I will be gone before sunrise. I'll pack my things and go!"

The Old Woman rose from her chair shakily and shouted for her servant girls. They quickly responded, each standing on either side ready to help raise her up. "You will not be leaving. You have no travel papers." She said this to him, as she stood in the doorway.

David stood up too, and as he did three men came around the corner, one carrying a torch. At her command, the man holding the torch took a white envelope from inside his shirt and held it to the torch. It immediately caught fire.

Recognizing that the envelope was what he used to keep travel papers and passport together, David launched himself from the porch, only to be caught and held by the other two men. He saw sheets of folded papers catch and curl into blackness. He watched helplessly as his authorization to leave the country burn, and when the envelope was beyond salvage, the two men released their hold.

Father fell to the ground.

Standing up slowly with the aid of her two servant girls on either side of her, she paused at the teak doorway and said, "Neither China, nor I, will ever let you leave again," her venomous voice husky and low. The Old Woman disappeared into the darkness of her house.

Quite as suddenly as the men appeared, David found himself alone in the dimness of nightfall. The only sounds were of the summer insects and his own pounding heart. How was he to get back to America? How long had his grandfather conspired with his estranged wife to get him and keep him here? And what about Laura back in California? How safe would she and his children be without him to protect them? If he was now a prisoner, would Grandfather throw his wife out of the house he owned? Where could she go? Her own family would not take her in. He moaned at the very thought of it, and his heart overflowed with grief and regret. He now understood how naive he was in believing all was forgiven and made right between himself and his grandfather and Uncles. He fell into their hands, and now the trap was sprung, leaving him helpless.

He wondered if he could take his chances and just walk (or run) away now. Could he convince an American-bound ship to take him without papers? What of the American consulate? Did China even have an American embassy, and how could he find it so far from city life? His head really hurt now.

After several hours, feeling the cramp of sitting on the ground, David pulled himself up. No longer feeling an inclination to run into the night, he went inside to lie down on his soft bed. He had been tricked by subtle subterfuge and he fell into a fitful sleep vowing that he would use the same deceptions upon his perpetrators. His last thoughts before falling into that tormented sleep were a vow of revenge and escape the quickest way possible.

Chapter 21

It had now been two months since her husband left, and one month since not receiving any correspondence or word from him. Laura was now in her seventh month of pregnancy, and her firstborn daughter demanded a great deal of her time and attention. Although she didn't have to, Laura regularly went into the restaurant more for the company than to work. Between the cook Sam and his wife Marjorie and their two young waitresses, Laura Mae did not have much to do, but she was grateful they gave her a little bit to do just to keep her mind off her missing husband. She waddled back and forth filling the shelves with stock and filling the salt and pepper shakers. She also hoped Harry might come into the restaurant and explain what her husband was doing.

She did not want to actually call his grandfather Harry to ask if he had heard from David. The man still frightened her. Harry paid their bills routinely and without question. She had money for groceries and to buy little things for her baby. In this regard, she was grateful for David's family and their support of her during his absence, but she didn't want to cross that invisible line that warned her off from calling Harry and speaking to him directly.

Laura kept busy with the usual and the mundane and felt a moment of relief on the day the phone rang at home. It was Harry. "How you? How the baby?" He questioned her. "We're fine, but I haven't heard from David in several weeks. Have you heard anything?" She asked him.

"Yes! Yes. News from David. I like to come over and tell you news, things you need to know about David. Is okay I come?" He asked her.

"Oh, yes. I'm dying to hear about him and especially when he is coming home." Laura answered. "He is all right, isn't he? Nothing's wrong, is it?"

"No, nothing wrong now. No wrong. Husband well," Harry replied.

"Would you like to come for dinner?" She asked, secretly hoping he would not.

"No…no. I come after dinner, yes? Tonight, about seven, yeah?" Harry said. His voice sounded chipper and cheerful as always as though she could imagine his toothy grin.

Waiting for the clock to reach the hour of seven, Laura was nervous. Was the house clean enough? Baby toys were on the floor, stacks of clean cotton diapers were folded on the dining room table, and a few baby bottles could be seen, but this was acceptable, wasn't it? She secretly feared deep down that nothing she could ever do would be right for such a man as Harry Yee. She tried for David's sake to embrace him, after all it did appear that things were going well for them as a result of his grandfather's support. But Laura remained guarded.

She decided to put a kettle of water on to boil for tea. She had some Chinese black tea she knew her husband liked and thought perhaps Harry might enjoy a cup as well. In the living room her baby daughter amused herself in her crib with all her toys. She had been fed, bathed and in another hour, would be given her night bottle and placed in her own bed.

Laura found some sugar cookies in her tin in the cupboard and placed four on a small glass plate. Just as she set the cookie plate on the dining room table, a rather quiet knock at the door caught her attention. She glanced at her living room wall clock; the minute hand just ticked to straight up seven o'clock. *"How punctual,"* she thought to herself as she moved to answer the door.

Harry stood, somewhat nervously, as he peered around her into her living room. Was he checking to see if she was alone? "Hee, hee! These for you, Missy," he spoke, shoving a huge box of chocolates into her hands.

"Harry, it wasn't necessary…but, but thank you!" Laura responded. "Please. Please, come in."

Still looking around, Harry stepped forward. Once he spotted the baby, he made straight for her. He reached down, and the baby's arms reached up in the expectation of being lifted up. Harry brought the child out of her crib. Laura's first instinct was to stop him. This near-stranger had her baby! She moved to relieve him.

"Harry, be careful now. She's just eaten," Laura admonished. "Here, let me have her. She might throw up and ruin your suit."

Harry relinquished the baby. "She good girl…good baby!"

When their baby was a month, old there was much pressure by Harry to throw a party for David and Laura's first-born daughter. Harry threw a small but lavish one-month party in the true Chinese tradition. In ancient Chinese culture, if an infant was lucky enough to survive its first thirty days, the occasion was celebrated. Later, the tradition became what is now known as the *"red egg and ginger"* celebration. David tried to explain the significance of giving all the guests that came a red egg for prosperity, and "Lysee" or small red and gold envelopes filled with new money as a symbol of wealth. Gingered foods were served, and candied ginger sat in bowls at every table. Their daughter, in turn, on this special occasion, received a great deal of jewelry which Laura thought was too expensive for a baby. She received two small jade baby bracelets that quickly went into the mouth of her daughter as she lay in her bassinette. She got several pairs of small red, black and green jade stud earrings, which Laura had no intention of piercing her baby's ears to accommodate. But she couldn't decide if Harry's gift for her baby girl was the best or the worst in terms of baby gifts. Harry had given their daughter a 24-carat gold ring, sized for an adult hand, and a 24-carat matching coin pendant on a 22-carat yellow gold heavy chain. The gift was dazzling, but entirely inappropriate. Laura quietly decided to lock these valuables up until her daughter turned twenty-one years of age. The whole affair left Laura unnerved and annoyed.

Turning her attention back to her Father-in-Law, Laura asked Harry if he wanted some tea, as she walked down the hall with her baby toward the kitchen. The kettle was whistling.

Harry spotted the box of Chinese black tea and nodded approval. "Aw, yeah, yeah! Tea is good," but rather than waiting for her, he stepped in front of her, measured out three tablespoons of tea leaves into the waiting pot, and poured in the hot liquid. He stirred once and re-placed the lid of the tea pot. He picked up the pot and motioned with his hand for her to go in front of him. Laura turned to go into the dining room off the kitchen where the cups and cookies waited.

Harry and Laura sat down. Laura gave her baby a cookie while Harry waited for his tea to steep.

"I'm very anxious to hear about David. What is your news; what have you heard?" Laura asked, as she settled the baby into her lap and pushing the cookie plate out of the baby's reach.

"We have good news for you and good news for David,"

Harry offered.

"Yes?" Laura Mae felt anxious as she encouraged him to continue.

"You will become a rich woman," Harry told her as he began to pour his tea.

Puzzled, Laura continued to stare at him as he set his teapot down after pouring the liquid into two cups.

Harry reached into his inner suit pocket, and to her amazement brought out a stack of money that started with a hundred dollar bill on top. It was held together with a red rubber band.

"Dis for you," he said.

Laura did not touch it, but looked at him, the money, and back at him for an explanation.

"No…no! Is real for you. You take money. Go home, see family. Go anywhere you like. Dis ten thousand dollar," Harry said sipping his hot brew by inhaling it noisily.

After a moment, Laura asked, "What is this money for, Harry?"

Now you promise me you no get upset. Good news for David. No so good for you. Husband David not coming back to Gold Mountain. He stay in China. He no love you and baby anymore. He marry real wife…Chinese wife. He no come home to you." Harry's face was like a clown's face. He drew the sides of his mouth down into severe frown, tilted his head deeply down to one side, and looked up at her with big, huge sad puppy dog eyes and a protruding lower lip. Laura wanted to giggle at the routine, but her mind was trying to process what he just said to her in very poor English.

David was not coming home. David didn't love her and their baby anymore. David had married another woman?

Stunned into silence, Laura listened as Harry proffered more. "Dis money start new life for you. You go on find new husband. His voice was softer, gentler. "Find handsome Hollywood "*Gwailo*" man to love, not lowly Chinee boy. He no good for you."

Laura still didn't respond. She sat staring beyond Harry's head, her hands rubbing her large swollen belly. Harry picked up the bundle of money. "Ten Thousand find many white men. Good men for you."

David was not coming home. David didn't love her and their baby anymore. David had married another woman?

Laura's brain was frozen in time and space. Harry's broken English was an annoying chatter in her ear, like a bug that buzzed annoyingly around her head and all she wanted to do was swat the bug away.

Harry now stood up and carefully began to reach for Laura's baby. "Chinee baby girl not good for white woman. No man marry you with Chinee baby. You give to me; we raise her like we raise David. We adopt." Harry sat with a crooked smile; his mouth shaped around his big teeth. He motioned to her belly and added, "Yeah, bof babies."

When Harry's hands touched hers to take the baby away from her, Laura snapped back to attention. She tightened her grip on her baby, at the same time standing up so quickly she knocked her chair backwards. She turned and ran back to the kitchen, her daughter in the crook of her arm.

Harry was shocked for a moment but soon was on her heels, following her to the kitchen, all the while he repeated what he said earlier. "David no love you and baby. You find new husband. You find good white man, have more babies. This baby no good for you. No find white husband with daughter like this. Ten thousand..." Harry's voice was high and filled with pleading now.

Laura fell against the kitchen counter, next to the drainboard where her washed dishes sat air-drying. She felt trapped as she shifted her baby to her other arm, wrapping both arms around her child so that Harry could not get at her. Feeling this was not enough, feeling as though Harry threatened her and the baby, Laura's maternal instincts kicked in, and she felt the need to fight and defend.

Almost blindly, as Harry reached for her baby girl, Laura's hand reached down to the drainboard, and came up with a large Chinese meat cleaver. It was David's favorite butcher knife.

Harry saw Laura Mae raise the knife over her head, and he stopped, he froze, his eyes not leaving the raised-up knife in mid-air. He burst out in Chinese threats, turning quickly around, raising his hands over his neck to protect himself from possible blows and ran.

Laura Mae saw the upper hand and despite holding a baby and her large protruding pregnancy gave chase to the retreating bastard running in front of her. Harry ran and Laura pursued still holding the cleaver over her head and holding onto her baby daughter with the other arm.

Screaming now in between the string of Chinese words she did not understand, she chased Harry into the living room, where he quickly circled the coffee table and ran into the dining room area. He stopped on the other side of the dining table, putting a chair in front of him.

"You get the hell out of my house, you son-of-a-bitch," yelled Laura. She felt her heart pounding, her face was surely reddish-purple with rage and temper and she felt spittle fly with each word of *"son-of-a-bitch"* she let fly.

Standing opposite her, on the wrong side of the table, Harry felt trapped, and he danced side-to-side not knowing which way to run. He picked up the bundle of money, and weakly repeated himself, "You take money! Make you rich white woman!"

Wham! The meat cleaver came down hard right where Harry's hand had been. *"That's going to leave a mark,"* Laura thought to herself. Harry jumped back dropping the money back on to the dining table. "You are never to touch my child or come near me again, you understand old man?" Laura's throat burned as she spat out the words. This time Harry screamed like a little girl.

"Gwaipo!" "Gwaipo!"

The baby was startled at the level of noise, felt her 'mother's distress, and started to cry. Harry came around the table and headed for the front door. Laura left the knife firmly imbedded into her dining table and grabbing the bundle of money, ran after Harry who was reaching the door.

As soon as he opened the front door, Harry flew out, yelling words she clearly could not understand. Laura Mae came out on the porch seconds behind him, yelling at him over her baby's cries, while throwing the bundle of money toward Harry. She hit him square in his back.

"Aiieee!" Harry yelped. He saw the bundle hit the ground, turned quickly, stooped and retrieved his ten thousand dollars. "You crazy woman! You not fit to marry Chinese. You no good crazy."

"Get out of here. I never want to see you again. You come back here, and I'll finish the job and chop you into pieces. You understand me, old man! I'll kill you, if you come near me and my daughter again." Laura, her baby and her unborn baby stood a seething rage of supremacy, at last finding her voice over injustice.

Harry reached his car, and after several inconvenient seconds, managed to unlock his car door. Safely inside his car, Harry spat out a curse as he pounded the steering wheel. "*Jamniggatowah!*"

He started his engine and pulled away in jerky, hesitating and frightened movements.

Porch lights came on in the few houses on her street, and shadows of people could be seen through their parted curtains.

Laura sat down hard onto her porch steps, giving all her attention to her crying baby. Her hand ached. Her heart pounded. She hoped her unborn did not suffer from all that just transpired. She shushed her baby softly, gave her kisses, calming herself as she quieted her baby. She looked up and down the street. Harry was long gone.

What would she do now? Where could she go? Who could she trust or turn to? Fresh tears and new fears sprang up to engulf her.

Chapter 22

David woke up as usual, in a blue funk, miserable and heart-broken. He wasted an entire week threatening, screaming, yelling and pleading with his Ni-Ni to no avail. He watched her steel herself from his assaults, the cold expression of her face never changing, never wavering. No words moved her, no tears affected her, no threats harmed her. She sat as stone. Exhausted, David retreated from her presence. He had no place to go but to the neighboring village and to the small group of men who had become his friends during the installation of the village well. There, he found solace and understanding to a degree. They acknowledged, practically in unison, the awful power wielded by such an old woman. But, in the end, no one recommended standing up to her. For David, it did look impossible. Their support was a show of respect for him, but it was acknowledged that other than mutual sympathy, little else could be done.

David sank into a daily depression. No one could tell him where an American Embassy was. No one knew how to get new travel papers without proper authentication or permission from the village matriarch. No one had any sound advice or knowledgeable answers. These were poor country people indeed.

Silence now stood between him and his Ni-Ni. He avoided her company, leaving early, returning late, or sometimes choosing to sleep in the flat bed of the truck rather than going home at all. Could he write a letter to his wife? No one knew how to post a letter to another country without going through his Ni-

Ni. No one travelled through their village often enough to post a letter outside the village. And if he could get a letter through, what would he have to tell his wife? Would he tell her he was being held hostage, against his will? She was in no position, pregnancy included, to come rescue him.

The American Embassy probably would not rescue him either as an émigré, was he even entitled to be represented as an American citizen? Without his papers, he would have difficulty even proving to them who he was. Who was he kidding, he could not even find an Embassy – so far removed from civilization was this village.

He thought of stealing the truck and heading for Canton, but he had no money. The American dollars he carried with him were now part of the ashes, along with his travel papers and passport.

The Villagers were sympathetic and consoled him by telling him not to give up hope. Though it was rare, Europeans did come through their village once-in-a-while. Just ten months ago, several came through on their way to the high Himalayan Mountains. "Ten months!" David thought, as his stomach tightened painfully. *Ten months!* Thoughts of Laura plagued his mind and tore at his heart.

One evening, he saw the Old Woman sitting on the veranda, apparently wanting to speak to him. He tried to walk past her. "You will sit so that I may explain what is expected of you." She spoke.

It was more of a command than a request. He sat down, looking straight ahead. The hate for her was like sour vomit in his mouth.

"Next week, you are to be married. I have picked your bride from the Cheung Village. She is young and suitable for you.

"I am already married," came his terse reply.

"I repeat myself. Your so-called marriage to a white woman is of no consequence. You are in China, and you *will* take a Chinese wife. The bride price has already been paid, the wedding has been arranged, and you *will* be married!" Her wrinkled mouth moved these words out very quickly.

"I cannot have two wives!" He defended himself.

"Why not? Chinese lords have been doing this for centuries," she quipped. You are allowed many wives and many concubines. I see no difference in this. You will marry, or your white concubine will experience difficulty if you do not," she spat these words out in a coarse low voice.

The true meaning of this threat made David's blood freeze. The reality was that genuine harm could come to his wife and daughter just as she warned. He now understood the faces of his enemies, and they were the ones he used to call his Family. He knew his cousins would obey any instruction given by his grandfather and the five uncles. Laura could be in great danger!

"Who must I marry? When? He asked, his voice cold and controlled.

"Her name is Soong Bing Li. She is seventeen years old, the oldest daughter to a shopkeeper in the village. He is a prosperous man whose Family goes back generations, and she is a good and only daughter. She is pure, and most importantly, she is Chinese and knows how to be a good Chinese bride."

She turned to face him, "Your wedding will be on the date of the full moon, and we will celebrate three days, as is our custom."

Turning once again toward the setting sun, she continued, "A house will be constructed here in this village where you may both live. In the interim, you both shall share my roof until your house is finished. I will enjoy watching over your happiness."

Feeling as though he might be sick, David squeezed both fists tightly and stood up. "As you wish," he said, and left her as quickly as his feet could carry him.

The next few weeks was a blur to him. David met Soong Li, as she liked to be called, and her vast Family members, some of whom worked on the well with him. There was a traditional Chinese wedding, strange, ethereal in nature, and confusing for him. While he had witnessed many Chinese weddings, life in America had altered his understanding of such traditions, and those who helped him, coached him, and talked him through it, were pushy and short-tempered with him for forgetting so many Chinese traditions. This was no occasion for him to act like an American. With tears in his eyes, and a tightness in his throat, David allowed himself to be married to this seventeen-year-old Chinese stranger. Three days of celebration ensued; song, dance, performances and revelry abounded, but David's spirit had fled him. He stood among these people as a stranger, a non-entity and a cursed enemy. For three days, he did not speak, nor did he touch his new bride. On the fourth day, once the ceremonies had concluded, the firecrackers had all exploded, the dancers and singers and musicians retired, and all the villagers gone back to their homes, David was left alone with Soong Li.

She was beautiful. She was shy and demure. Her head stayed down, and her eyes never reached his. He stood as far away from her as he could arrange, sitting at the window smoking a cigarette.

Finally, she spoke. "Husband, you do not find me attractive?"

Without looking at her, David coughed, and said, "This has nothing to do with you. I am forced to marry you. I married you for the sake of my wife… my other wife." This was awkward.

"Our villages are small. I have heard your story. I understand why you married me, but you will not discover real freedom if you shame me in the process." Her voice was quiet, filled with respectfulness.

"What do you mean "shame you?" He asked.

Still looking down at her folded hands, she said, "It is expected that you lie with me and make me your wife. People…people are watching. If you do not, it will be a sign of rejection and I will be returned to my father in shame, and you, you will be left to deal with our matriarch."

David's bowels clenched. This mess was getting deeper and deeper, going from bad to worse. Now, he had sexual duties to perform like a puppet on somebody's string. He sighed. "I'm going for a walk," he told her, tossing his cigarette out the window. Before he stepped off the veranda, he turned to her and said, "Don't worry. You won't be returned to your father's house in shame." He walked away.

It was now one month into his marriage. David played the dutiful husband, did all that his Ni-Ni told him without complaint. He slept with his wife but had no feelings for her other than feeling responsible for her. He listened to her chatter and spoke in short words and never offered her information about America or his life there. He showed no emotion and offered no resistance. To do so may threaten the life of his true wife and children. He wasn't even sure that something terrible hadn't already happened to them. This far from home, how could he ever be certain? He missed Laura so very much. By his calculation, he had to assume Laura gave birth to their second baby, and his little daughter had a sibling baby brother or sister. He wondered if he would ever lay eyes on them again.

It was under a routine sun, under a routine day, when one of his closest acquaintances, Jong Li, offered him a cup of tea under the shade of a large banyan tree. "I have very good news, secret news!" He announced, handing David a cup of tea.

David was used to village gossip and found most of it dull and boring. Nothing really happened here. Pigs were stolen by angry or covetous neighbors. Dogs gave birth. Rumors about local politics and family feuds were typical conversation fare. David didn't expect to be impressed as he sipped his tea. He lit a cigarette, as his companion continued.

"She did not burn your papers," he said quietly.

There was a big pause. Did he hear right? Though his Chinese was getting better, he did not trust his ears.

"What did you say?" He demanded.

"She deceived you. She is a great actress, our Landlady. She did not burn your travel papers." There was a smirky smile on the man's face. Jong Li was clearly amused.

"Tell me all that you know," David pleaded, turning his body to fully face his Village friend.

"A-hem. She is a masterful manipulator. I have it on good authority from someone inside your home that she stole your envelope, switched out its contents, and hid them where you would not dare to search. She keeps your papers in case she must threaten you more. It is her only power over you."

Stunned, David sat in silence, contemplating this news.

Enjoying his role as revelator, the man continued, "She keeps these documents for her own sake, knowing their power over you. You must somehow find them and make your escape. Every escape requires a plan. Do you have a plan?" Jong Li chuckled.

The possibilities came flooding his mind so fast, he could not keep up with them all.

"Please tell me that you are not lying to me. I have more than enough heartache to deal with," David said, his eyes pleading.

"Not everyone here agrees with what has been done. Men are forced to do as dictated by others. We grew up kowtowing, yet many of us desire to be our own masters, our own landlords. We are quiet rebels who fight only in our minds. But you have made many friends here. We know you do not belong here. You American, not Chinese. Your fight must be real, and we are counting on you to somehow win. It would be a great victory for many of us, and I for one, would be grateful to witness your escape. What an adventure to tell my grandchildren one day!" Jong Li smiled broadly, taking a sip of satisfying tea.

His hopes raised; David began a foundation of an escape plan. He watched carefully from the deck of the house being built across from his 'grandmother's house. Village workers were slowly building a smaller version of her house for him and his new bride. From his vantage point, he watched the routine of the Old Woman's house, as he had done for five straight days. In that amount of time, he saw that she was punctual about getting up, eating, napping, and dining in the evening. She went to bed at the same time each night. The two servant girls were in constant attendance, unless they were sent on errands. The errands were typical; they bore messages to other houses, instructions for their field workers, invitations for tea to the fortune teller, and invitations to the female gossipers from each village. It was too difficult to move her. He needed to get inside her rooms to search for his papers, but how? He watched and waited. What he observed was people came to her, but she did not seem to ever leave the house herself. David's sense of urgency was fueled by the possibility that she could really destroy his travel papers at any time she wanted. He had to get inside and search!

It wasn't until he next met with his inscrutable friend in the neighboring village, who seemed to be very pleased with himself as he lit his pipe, his eyes twinkling.

"You soon will have your chance to flee, American," came his baited words.

"What do you mean?" David asked. "She never leaves. I can't get inside to search for my travel papers."

"Patience is wisdom, and being wise will keep you from being caught," he replied.

"Stop talking in riddles! And why do you smile so? You look like the cat that ate the canary." David's frustration made him short.

"'The cat that ate the canary?' Hmmm! You are right! I have just digested very good information indeed. You should know I am a cunning cat to eat this canary," he chortled.

David would not bite his bait. He just hunched over, slumping in frustration. His friend continued, still pleased with himself.

"You are unaccustomed with our local celebrations, and as it is the end of our harvest season, you do not know that we have a customary celebration heralding the end of harvesting, and the coming of our Full Moon. We also agree to match young ones in marriage and establish bride prices for the peasant workers. We also bring our annual grievances to the attention of our landlord, who will judge each circumstance and make rulings for restitution."

"I've been here almost eleven months, and you people seem to celebrate everything."

"It is true, we enjoy music, good food, wine and firecrackers. But you miss my point, Young One."

"Which is?"

"Your Grandmother must attend; she is to judge our annual grievances. It is her duty, and she never fails in her duty. This celebration brings her out of her house, and into this Village, where all can attend from all neighboring villages. She will be gone for hours."

His eyes sparkled with pleasure as he puffed a great deal on his clay pipe.

"She will be gone for hours!" David repeated this information and jumped up from his seat.

"She will be gone for hours!" He yelled now, and grabbed Jong Li, forcing him to dance with him while he repeated the words, "She'll be gone for hours! Ha-ha!"

David was ecstatic! This was his chance. Letting go of his friend who fell back hard and dizzy onto their stone bench, he asked for pertinent details. When was this celebration? When would it be considered over, and when would she return to her house? If he found his papers right away, how could he make his escape before her return? What would she likely do if she learned that he left? Would she likely send men after him? How could he out-run pursuers? What would he do if he couldn't find his precious papers?

Jong Li calmed him down and told him to be ready at the end of the week, the day of the harvest moon. He held up four fingers and told him four days. He said he would arrange for the only truck between both villages to be parked nearby. Without this truck, no one would likely pursue him, even on horseback. The only other motorized vehicle belonged to the Christian missionaries several Villages over, and he had knowledge that theirs was currently on blocks awaiting the delivery of new tires from the city. The only task David needed to focus on was waiting for the Old Woman and her servants to leave, and to find his documents, make it to the truck to be left in the upper field near the road, and leave. It was a simple and brilliant plan.

David found it difficult to sleep, eat or concentrate on the building of his house. The simple plan of escape was played repeatedly in his mind. The search scenario and the escape played out like a looped piece of film trapped in his head. He did his best to appear calm and dutiful in his daily routines to prevent arousing suspicion. On the morning of the festival, he was to meet once again with his Village friend to make sure their plans had not changed.

Finally, that morning arrived, and as he was about to take his walk to meet his friend, a servant girl approached and kowtowed.

"She who is my Mistress commands your presence, Honorable Son," she said, not looking up at him.

"When?" He asked her.

She hesitated, bowed to him again, and said, "Now, if you please," came her reply.

David was annoyed, not wanting to talk to the Old Woman ever again. But he motioned for the girl to lead the way and found himself walking toward the house behind her.

The Old Woman was ensconced in her throne-like teak chair. She sipped on a cup of tea, eyes staring out to her fields. "Tonight, is an important celebration, and as my successor, you must begin to learn our traditions. We celebrate the first Full Moon at end of harvest, and there is much decisions to be made for the farm workers and other villagers. Since I make all the decisions here, you will attend me and observe. You may well have to do this for all future Moon festivals. The villagers expect much of my wisdom, and you must learn how it is done." She paused to sip her tea. Placing her cup down on the residing table, she continued. "You and your wife will attend the evening. You will ride with me when the truck comes to pick us up, and you will sit on my right-hand side at the judgment chair."

He was stunned. He never thought he would be required to attend, much less sit by her side throughout the entire evening. How would he excuse himself? There would be no excuse that would allow him to escape her presence long enough to go five miles back and search her house. How stupid was he? He felt like running away right now.

"Ni-Ni, I – I am not sure I can attend," he said weakly. "I-I think I am coming down with an illness, my stomach…" He held his hands to his stomach.

"Nonsense! I shall send my servant over with some ginger tea, and you will rest for the afternoon. No work. Tell the carpenters to go home so that you can rest. You will attend, even if your stomach still offends. This is important to me, now go and rest. Tea will be sent over."

He understood the tone of her voice. He was dismissed and was not to say another word for fear of a larger argument he could not win. He turned and left for the partially framed house. He sent the carpenters home for the day and waited for his tea. When the ginger tea came, he drank it, and told his wife he needed to walk to clear his head. He left making his way down the road as quickly as he could.

David and Jong Li, indeed the closest friend he had right now, agreed to meet between the villages a few miles out near the new well they had worked together on. There was an outcropping of rocks above the terraced rice paddies where they could watch for others below them and not be over-heard talking. He was contently waiting for David as he approached.

Sensing David's anxiety, he suggested he light a cigarette before he talked to calm himself. David's hands shook as he lit the fag.

"I feel so stupid. I never imagined that she would demand that I sit in judgment with her all night long. She wishes to teach me my responsibilities when I take over for her. Stupid! Stupid! How can I get away now?" David did not get a satisfying calm from his cigarette and tossed it into the rice paddy below. His hands held his head as he slumped down beside his quiet friend. Their silence was nearly palpable. Finally, his friend spoke.

"This evening demands great sacrifice if we are to succeed," he said. David only looked up pleading for him to continue this line of thought. "I have a plan," his friend announced with firmness.

Hours later, the sun began to set as David washed and dressed in silk embroidered robes. He took his Chinese wife by the arm and guided her to the truck where the dowager was already ensconced on her teak chair, sitting in the middle of the truck's flat bed. Two strong young men stood one on either side of her chair holding a rod that ran through guides at the back of her chair enabling them to lift her and her chair, and to stabilize her as the truck moved along the bumpy, uneven country dirt road. He noticed the dowager sat on many pillows, and pillows were stuffed under her bony arms and her frail back, offering her a cushioned ride over bad terrain. David deposited first his wife, and then himself, as their driver proceeded to the nearby village.

This village had a large square which held a stage approximately eighteen inches from the ground, and appropriately placed the dowager and her Family above all the others who gathered around the stage. Since it would be a long night of complaints and requests, celebrations of the harvest were held at the opposite end of the village, and at the town square, a queue of people were lining up to kneel before the old woman.

Food and drink had been set out and refreshed from time to time by servants and townspeople.

David saw that each visitor came to the old lady on their knees, perhaps out of respect, but more than not, out of fear of retribution, he thought. After hearing the sixth complaint of *"he said," "she said,"* and other pithy accusations, David looked at the long line and groaned inside. How would he escape and return to his village? How?

Just then, he saw his friend and the young boy, the thirteen-year-old who had driven him to the well and back each day, were approaching the stage. David's heart beat faster. He was sure "The Plan" was about to unfold.

Between his friend Jong Li and the young boy who would be Clark Gable was a huge platter upon which sat a darkly roasted baby pig. Its glazed body glistened in the lantern lights. They both bowed their heads at the foot of the stage and interrupted the kneeling petitioner.

"Honorable Lady, Honorable First-born Son, we offer you the first fruits of harvest. This pig has been roasting all day in your honor. May we approach?" His friend asked.

"Give it to my grandson to carve up," she said, slightly annoyed at the interruption.

The two conspirators carried the heavy tray up on the stage and took David back behind his grandmother where a large carved blade was produced. The tray of pork was put down on a low table. Their backs were all that were visible to the crowd.

"Give me your hand," his friend whispered, as he rummaged in his coat pocket.

"What," David asked, confused. "Which hand?"

Pulling a frustrated face, his friend did not answer, but grabbed David's nearest hand, his left hand. In nearly one quick motion, his friend took the carved knife and cut David across the palm of his hand, then took from his pocket a large cloth already dripping with blood and stuffed it into David's slightly bleeding palm. At the same time, David yelped in genuine pain and surprise. His friend did indeed cut his hand!

"Mistress, an honest mistake! Do not punish me! We must get him to a healer. The wound is very deep." His friend grabbed one arm and the thirteen-year-old grabbed David's other arm.

David was tempted to look at his wound, the cloth dripping blood on the stage as they moved to confirm how deep it was. It only stung him with surprise. "Mistress! A mistake! We must hurry and bind his wound!"

His grandmother saw the bloody cloth covering his hand, saw the dripping dots of blood wetting the stage in small red pools, and her eyes widened in horror. "What damage have been done to his hand? What has happened?" She demanded.

"The knife is sharp, it slipped in his hand, Mistress. We must take him to a healer and bind it quickly to stop the bleeding," his friend said, pulling on David's arm this way and that, sending more drops of blood to spatter around her chair.

His wife jumped up and attempted to check his hand, but he motioned her back. Understanding the ruse, for the cut was not that deep, and this was certainly not his blood, David aided his friend's plan. "Grandmother, the cut is very deep. I must be stitched at once. I will be returned before too long. Let me go to the healer."

"Take him in the truck and see that you return him within the hour. I will not stand for this on such an important night as this! Return him quickly." She cried out, waving a dismissive hand to them.

David, his friend, and the young boy raced off the stage and toward the truck, as his friend dramatically yelled, "I am sorry Master, please forgive any offence. It was an accident. An accident!" Jong Li cried out.

When David got to the safety of the truck, the young boy started the engine, and pulled away from the village, David took off the bloody bandage and saw a small angry but very shallow line across his palm. It stung but clearly did not need stitches. He smiled at his friend and then the boy.

"Pig's blood." His friend said. "I told you this evening would require great sacrifice, and the little pig gave his life's blood for your escape. If all goes well, you will find your documents quickly and leave for Canton immediately. No one can follow us, for there is no other transportation."

David was beaming, and then his face melted as deeply hidden emotions came to the surface. He started to cry. The truck cab was awkwardly silent until his friend, his genuine and true friend, spoke again, this time softly. "We made sure the truck's gas tank has been fueled, there is food and water hidden in a basket in the back. Do not worry, my friend. You will escape this night. No one will pursue us. Your escape will be unhindered, and so that you do not get lost, Cheung Lao Yee will drive you all the way to the boat docks in Canton.

David straightened his head and shoulders and drew a deep breath, using his fingertips stained with pig's blood to wipe his eyes and cheeks. He looked at the smiling teen whom he had always called "Boy" and understood.

"Aren't you coming, as well?" he turned and asked Jong Li. If you remain, she may take my escape out on you and your Family," David said.

"She will not," he replied. "They will return, hours later, carrying the dowager in her chair the entire five kilometers, and find me tied up and unconscious."

David smiled and the boy Cheung grinned. They set their eyes on the road ahead. David's thoughts raced with anticipation. He would find his papers; he would purchase passage on the first ship leaving port, even if it was not headed to America. He would leave China immediately, to any country which would eventually take him back to the United States. As soon as they reached Canton, he would stay only if it required before leaving China one last time. He wanted out of this God-forsaken country and as far from the reach of his grandmother as he could arrange. He would also send a telegram to his wife to quietly get out of town immediately that her life might be in danger. He would not wait for her reply and he would tell her he was on his way back home to leave word with Sam and Marjorie where she could be found. He would telephone her as soon as he cleared customs in either Los Angeles or San Francisco.

Laura. Laura. Laura. His heart ached for her.

Chapter 23

David had been out to sea for six days now. He drew hard on his cigarette before snuffing the hot ash out in the tray that sat beside his small bed. He slipped his arm behind his head and stared up the familiar metal ceiling painted a disgusting and dirty yellow. To him it was beautiful. The sea outside was calm and the ship swayed smoothly as it coursed toward the Philippines. He had been out to sea for almost a week, stopping in Taiwan, Japan and Malaysia, picking up and dropping off crates of product destined for parts unknown. He was among five other non-laboring paid passengers headed for the United States. It was a working cargo ship, which took on a few paying passengers filling the few guest accommodations the ship had. If you could call these cramped, dingy cabins accommodations. David did not mind. He was all smiles.

He boarded this freighter because it was the only one ship prepared to leave China the next day, and he nearly didn't make it on board altogether.

It was easy for him to reflect on the last few days in China, now that he was safely on board this ship called *The China Sea*.

As soon as his friend and the boy had arrived back in his village, David ran to change clothes, dropping his silk embroidered coat on the dirty ground. He slipped on his linen slacks, pulled on a clean pair of socks and slipped on his leather street shoes. He felt their pinch as he laced them up quickly, ignoring the fact that he hadn't worn leather shoes in the eleven months he had been here. His feet objected to their confinement, and the steam of his environment apparently shrunk the leather a bit. He grabbed a small grip throwing in two shirts, another pair of pants, his shaving kit and his slippers and all the underwear he could find. After putting on a clean shirt, he found his watch with the leather band, formerly too hot to wear in this weather. The watch, a Bulova Laura gave him at their last Christmas, was set to California Pacific Standard Time. It was seven p.m. in the evening where she was at. He was reluctant to change to other time zones as he traveled because he always wanted to know the time of day it was for Laura. He took his bag and ran out of his room, finding his friend and Cheung picking carefully through the sitting room.

"My papers 'have to be in her room." David said dropping his bag and running toward her rooms at the back of the house, his friends close behind.

Kerosene lamps lined three walls. Matches lie on an entry table, and the young boy grabbed them and began lighting each lamp. Soon, the room was ablaze in light to see by. They stood in awe for a few seconds, never having witnessed her private room, the room of a Lady Dowager. David had not been in this private sanctuary since he was a young boy. He was the first to snap out of this hesitation, and he began to rifle through the nearest black lacquered vanity that held many drawers and sat low to the ground. The other two woke up and began to take different corners. They were silent, not speaking a word as they carefully poked the privacy of their matron.

David moved from the vanity table to her side tables which held some books, herb bottles, wooden boxes and decorative hair pieces. Nothing here was large enough to hold cash and papers. He next turned to her bed which was an ornate cupboard, really.

Lifting the heavy mattress to displace the bedding under her multiple pillows. Nothing. He angrily ripped the entire mattress off the bed hoping to reveal a secret place. His two friends gathered at the mattress to help him tear through it. Cheung began lifting her curtains that surrounded the bed frame to make sure nothing was behind the heavy dark curtains, while David destroyed the mattress. Nothing.

They stood still for a moment, breathing heavily and looking frantically around to access what they might have overlooked. Nothing was apparent. They were frustrated and baffled. What if his travel papers were given to another person away from this village beyond his reach and identification?

David spotted a set of familiar canes in the corner of her room. He knew these canes. She had one daily and used it to poke her servants, point accusingly at him and others and leaned on these canes to bear up her miserable old bones. He ran and grabbed the thickest one and began to beat the surfaces of her room. He used it to scrape things from their surfaces. They spilled. They crashed and broke into many pieces. Her things flew through their air and tumbled down opposite walls. He was yelling, screaming really. His anger coated the room as he swung the cane and systematically demolished the entire place.

With or without his papers he intended to leave, but first in destroying this room, he would break free his heart from the grip of her terror and reign over him. He did to her room what he wanted to do to her frail old body. He wanted her to die.

All three looked around. A large wooden chest crashed in all the rage and lay in pieces on the floor. Jewelry spilled out among the shattered wooden drawers. She had many rings, long ropes of jade in all colors, some tiny earrings, some Chinese coins, but no papers.

"Help me move the bed," David instructed. All three approached the heavily curtained and large wooden bed. It sat about three feet off the floor and was nearly six feet square with a heavy canopy and side curtains that closed the occupant in from all sides. It was beautiful, hand-carved and appeared to be very old. David did not intend to be delicate in handling the bed of a dragon. He meant to tip it over. He wanted to search underneath it. The three dragged the bed away from the wall, but before David could get behind it to push it over, Cheung cried out.

"Look!" He pointed up at the canopy.

As they pushed the bed away from its wall, the material of the curtained ceiling began to sway in a conspicuous manner. The black material sagged in the middle, as though weighted down with something. Cheung leapt upon the bed frame and pulled on the canopy fabric until it yielded and tore. A small bundle fell through the widening hole as the fabric gave way. David's travel papers, tied with a red silk cord, fell almost directly at his feet.

In one fluid motion David picked up the bundle. There was his cash, about $500 U.S. dollars, his passport, his visa papers and a letter of intent to travel signed by Harry Yee. It was all there. Everything he needed to return home again. The three all registered at the same time and ran. David yelled. "Wait!" He turned and ran back to her room.

Though no one was chasing after them that he could figure, and though no one could run the five miles to stop him in time, he nevertheless felt an urgency to leave. But he wanted to take more than what he had with him. He wanted proof that this happened to him. He wanted evidence to show Laura what he had to do to escape. He bent down on the ground and picked through the Dragon Lady's jewelry. It didn't matter the value of the jewelry or what looked more expensive than the other, he merely wanted tokens to take back to his wife. He selected two rings. One was a black onyx stone, cut in a flat square set with diamonds all around its gold base. The other was a jade stone shaped in a small narrow diamond shape, set in pure yellow gold. He remembered this ring being on her wrinkly fingers from when he was a little boy. When he entered the outer room again, he threw the two rings into his travel bag.

Outside, as he tossed his bag into the front seat of the truck, his friend and Cheung were grabbing some rope.

"Over here," Jong Li shouted, moving up a small hill to a nearby tree. "Tie me to this tree." Having said that, he took a small branch off the tree and began tearing his own skin on his face, making small tears, and grimacing at the pain he was causing. He reached into his pocket and smeared pig's blood on his face, mingling a bit of his own blood with the animal who gave its life for this cause. The effect looked as though he was brutally beaten.

"It will look as though you overtook me in a fight." He said to the others. "Here, Cheung, take my coat. Bury it a hundred miles from here. I have no excuse for all that blood in my pocket."

Cheung took the coat, but before ropes could tie down his friend, David grabbed him, and held him wordlessly. He had no words to tell his friend how much this meant to him. But before long, his friend forced him back. "You are destined for other things, great Lord. Go home to the Gold Mountain and never return here. I will tell my grandchildren great tales of how a suckling pig and an old fool helped you escape."

"What of me? Will you tell how I helped him run away?" Cheung asked brightly.

"Yes, I will speak of you also. It will be a great story, a great story indeed. Now, you must go. She may have sent runners looking for us."

This made the trio move to action and they set upon David's friend to tie him sturdily to the trunk of the tree, making sure he was as comfortable as possible. Taking the bloodied coat, they waved good-bye to their inconvenienced co-conspirator, and boarding the truck, took off down the dusty road. And though he wished to be far, far down the road David cautioned Cheung not to be reckless or drive too fast for fear of breaking down before they could truly escape.

Meanwhile, Laura stood at the front door of Dr. Eugene Dong's large white house. The door was big and impressive. She had always visited the doctor in his small office to the side and rear of his property. She had never approached the front of home before but this was Sunday, and his Office was closed, and Laura was taking the chance he would be home. Despite her nervousness, she knocked on the door. Within a short minute, a female Negro servant dressed in a black uniform with a crisply ironed white apron opened the door.

"Yes, may I help you?" She asked.

"I – I need to speak with Doctor Dong, please. Tell him it's urgent," Laura said, wringing her hands.

"Will you come inside and wait, while I speak to the doctor?" The servant said in a low and polite tone.

Laura entered the foyer and immediately sat down in a chair next to a large ornate breakfront. The house was indeed immense and very immaculate. The decorations, at least in this part of the room, were very pricey Asian artifacts. Laura wondered if she had made a mistake coming here.

Before her nerves forced her to bolt from the room, Eugene

Dong entered the foyer, and the Negro servant who followed him turned and started downstairs to her quarters.

"Laura, how nice to see you again. Is everything all right? Is there trouble with the pregnancy?" He came forward and took her by both her hands as she stood before him.

"Dr. Dong, I am in terrible trouble and must speak with you," she said, her eyes glistening with coming tears.

"Tell me first, are you in any physical pain? Are you hurt in anyway?" He asked her.

"No. No! I am perfectly healthy. I am in great trouble though," she quickly answered.

"Come this way then." He led her by her elbow to the sitting room beyond, stopping at the stairwell, he called down, "Ruby, please bring a tea tray to the lounge."

In a short while, Ruby brought in a beautiful silver tea set, intricately carved and beyond elegant. The little cakes and pieces of fruit went untouched, as Laura placed her hot porcelain China cup and saucer down on the marble table in front of her.

The words burst out of her as though she no longer could contain them. She talked rapidly, returning to parts of her story over and over. Her hands flew in patterns as she spoke. The handkerchief she had palmed was pulled, tugged and stressed as she held it tightly. At the end she held the handkerchief and one hand over her eyes as her head dropped.

"So, here I am with no place to go, seven months pregnant, and a toddler in tow. I don't know if what Harry told me is true, if David really did abandon me, our marriage, his children, and if he married someone else. I have no way of finding out. I don't even really know where he is in China. I'm not sure I even have family or friends who would take me in while in this condition. I can't work in this way, and I can't stay anywhere in town where

Harry can find me. Everyone I know will love nothing more than to tell me 'I told you so' rather than take me in." Her hands fretted.

Dr. Dong took a long drink of his tea and set his cup down before he spoke. "You did the right thing, Laura, coming to me. I, of course, have my resources and can possibly verify Harry's story. I might even be able to find your husband, given some time." He paused.

"I insist that you and your child stay here with me. I have plenty of room, and you are in no condition to travel away from here in your present condition. To do so may compromise your pregnancy and bring an earlier than expected labor. It won't exactly be premature birth, but we do not want to invite early labor, do we? Where is your baby girl now?"

"I've been staying at Sam and Marjorie's small apartment. In their tiny living room. My baby is with them." Laura responded.

Laura expressed to him her concerns that Harry might show up at the restaurant to threaten Sam and Marjorie into telling them where she and her baby were. She also expressed fear of what reprisals might be levied toward her friends, and even Dr. Dong himself. She knew the Chinese community respected Dr. Dong greatly, but would Harry feel powerful enough to come after him to get to her? He, after all, wanted to take her children away from her.

"I know Harry and Harry's syndicate. He is a profiteer and a gambler. He pays off the police and commits crimes against the laws of this land with his gambling houses and his prostitution. He's a 'two-bit criminal' as they say in the movies. I do not fear him, but for your sake and the sake of your babies, I will have my house watched. I, too, have my resources," he reminded her confidently.

Dr. Dong placed his hands on her shoulders to reassure her. Then he excused himself from the lounge and retreated to inform his wife of his intentions. He promised to return shortly, and when he came back, they would immediately go to Sam and Marjorie's apartment to fetch her suitcases and her baby daughter. Laura sat and quietly cried while she waited for the good doctor's return.

David and Cheung had reached Canton three days later, driving intensely throughout the night until exhaustion and distance had reined in their fears. They realized they were far enough to stop and sleep and eat and refresh themselves properly, and they could drive more slowly. They buried the pig-blood-soaked coat, and David's palm was already healing, and he now sported a light brown scab over the surface of his hand. He tied a clean handkerchief over it to keep out the dirt.

At first, David's countenance was angry and sour. It took a few days for him to catch the excitement and enthusiasm of his travel partner. Cheung asked incessant questions about the Gold Mountain, and David would politely respond. Somewhere, in his mind, his thoughts projected forward. Would he find Laura and his babies well? If anything had happened to them, what would he be able to do to Harry? To Jimmy? To all the uncles and cousins who threatened and ultimately betrayed him? And if Laura was still there, would she be able to understand what happened here in China? Would she forgive him for taking another wife? The whole thing was still a fresh nightmare for him. Never-ending nightmares.

Cheung's chatter was a welcomed distraction and David allowed his spirit to lean on this youth and his excitement so that he wouldn't fall into greater depression. The sights and smells of Canton enlivened both their spirits, and they went immediately to the boat docks. They spoke to the Harbor Master, getting the names of the ships taking on passengers, and their destinations, and most importantly the times each ship would be leaving port. For David, it was sooner the better, but for Cheung, it was different.

After finding out all they needed from the Harbor Master, they left to go to the marketplace to find food and travel clothing. David had some clothing, but no jacket, and Cheung came with all he wore and nothing else.

They ate rich foods, enticing roasted meats, succulent sweet and juicy fruits and juices, and indulged their bellies before setting out for tailor shops. But before they left the market stalls, they checked their funds and found David's cash would most certainly return him to California, but it was not enough to get Cheung there as well. They decided to sell the truck rather than abandon it on the piers.

Cheung ran up and down the marketplace yelling, "A fine motor truck for sale," and "it can haul many, many goods to market." The truck gathered many interested parties and after turning on the engine and allowing a few passengers to sit behind the wheel, the bidding began. In the end, a merchant paid cash in an abundant amount where others could not. Cheung had his travel funds.

They returned to the docks, and each purchased their boat tickets. One ticket for David, leaving seven a.m. the next morning on the *"The China Sea,"* and the other ticket was for Cheung on *"The Madagascar,"* an African freighter leaving for several European countries, the coast of Africa and eventually San Francisco. Cheung chose the ship because it had an English-speaking crew and he wished to learn all he could during the trip and secondly, the departure date would allow him to make the most of his time in Canton which had one movie house and so much more to see and experience. Cheung thought that if he were to never return to China, he wanted more memories of it than just his tiny village life and now he had a chance to see much more of the world as well. David was sorry to be parted from Cheung, but he would not delay his departure from China. He had to leave and Cheung understood. They would meet again; he had promised him.

Cheung accompanied David to the docks the next morning, dressed in high travel fashion. David had helped him pick out a tailored linen suit with brown suspenders, a silk shirt, tie and socks, and a white straw fedora. The brown slip-on leather shoes were beautiful but hurt his feet because he had gone barefoot most of his life. He bought a new pair of Chinese slippers to give him some relief from the hard street shoes. He purchased a leather suitcase and loaded it with a new shirt, slacks, underwear and toiletries. David purchased a warmer jacket knowing the weather in America would be cooler.

They said their goodbyes in front of the customs office, David giving Cheung quick and hurried instruction about not trusting anyone, and to be very secretive and careful about all the money he had. He cautioned Cheung about robbers and thieves and unscrupulous people who would destroy him for his money and Cheung smiled and patted David's arm with assurances that he would be careful. For Cheung, the world was now his, and he wanted to taste it all. After saying their goodbyes, he was heading to the movie house to see an American film starring a man called Humphrey Bogart. David worried that the money would evaporate before he even reached America. Cheung merely tipped his new fedora hat, feeling and looking on top of the world, as he turned and left David in the customs line.

David's thoughts returned to home and Laura. He could see in the far distance, the busying of crew preparing his ship, "*The China Sea*" for departure. He was itching to be aboard. He finally reached the counter of the customs officers, and he handed over his travel papers.

On their shopping spree the previous day, David took advantage of the marketplace to purchase a few gifts he hoped to sugarcoat his return to his real wife. He purchased a beautiful set of porcelain China, complete with tea pot, cups, saucers, plates, and bowls. The pattern was beautiful blue to match Laura's eyes. He also purchased two baby-sized Chinese silk pajama sets and the most important gift of all, a diamond ring. It was a beautiful one-carat round diamond set in a heavy decorative square in a raised setting. It was his desire to propose to Laura all over again, on bended knee, to beg her forgiveness and accept this ring. When they married, he could only afford a plain thin gold band. Now she would have a wedding set.

His mind was going over these images when the uniformed guard at the counter asked him to step in the office. David was not expecting this. He wanted to have his papers stamped and be allowed to board the ship like the others before him. The clock on the wall indicated six thirty a.m. The ship would leave in one half hour.

David picked up his small crate of dishes and his grip and stepped into the small guard shack. It had but one small window and was dark and somewhat dirty. A fat man in uniform sat behind a desk with a motorized fan blowing into his sweaty face.

The guard standing next to the desk took David's grip and began to rummage through it, putting the items on the table next to the fat man's desk. The man behind the desk questioned him about being the only Chinese on board this ship, and for what reason. He was neither a merchant nor a businessman. David gave him his grandfather's letter attesting to his travel purposes as business for his grandfather's interests.

"Yet, all you travel back with are a small set of dishes and baby clothes." The fat man countered. David did not confess to the diamond ring, or the other two rings that were secreted in his jacket pocket that hung folded on his arm. He held that tightly against him. David told him a lie that other purchases had been shipped out on another ship already days earlier.

"Where are the manifests for those goods? Can you prove that?" The man asked.

David could not. David told him the manifests were given to his grandfather's agent who had already left for San Francisco. "What was this agent's name?" What was the name of the company he worked for?"

David's thoughts raced. What if he were detained? What if he could not leave China because he lacked proof he was on business for his grandfather? Worse, what if he was jailed? The clutches of his nightmares tightened their grip on him, and he began to sweat like the fat man behind the desk.

David placed all his papers in front of the fat man and pleaded to leave. His wife and child had not seen him in many months. His wife was expecting another child who could be born already. David's emotions were genuine.

The fat man considered this and then sat forward looking over David's papers. David prayed to an unknown god. In another swift motion, the fat man lifted his stamp and stamped his documents handing them back to David, telling him to go. David picked up his grip and lifted the small crate of dishes.

"Leave those there," the fat man barked.

Without hesitation, David put the crate of dishes down again and ran from the office. He knew he had minutes before the gang plank would be hauled away from the ship's side. The dishes were a small price to pay for his release. He made his final escape with two sets of baby pajamas and three rings hidden in his inside jacket pocket. It could have been worse, but when David watched the ship finally push away from the dock, safely on board at last, he could not help but curse the land he was leaving and most of its people.

The Final Chapter

This is where I sum things up. Here is where all the loose ends get neatly cut away, and the frayed ends cauterized.

Henry Fong did locate my father many years later as an adult when we lived in Hayward, California. Their reunion was a happy one, and one that took nearly thirty years to become a reality. Both agreed that the Yee Family did horrible things, much akin to slavery, and that their lives were far better once they decided as adults to stay far away from the influences of the five uncles. Neither knew the whereabouts of Daniel, and neither ever heard nor saw him again.

As children, we were often dragged to Uncle Jimmy's Oakland restaurant, called "The Right Way Cafe", a cafe that served Chinese-American food. Dad took us because he could feed his now six children for free and catch up on family gossip in the back kitchen. Dad learned to cook hanging out and working in Jimmy's restaurant. The atmosphere was much more different for his six of us children. We did not speak Chinese, but as we ate, the "Chicken" women, as we called them, would slowly gather around our table. They talked loudly in Chinese, occasionally pointing to us, and laughing as they smirked, clucked their tongues and gossiped. They tugged at my sister's curly hair and made fun of my brother's hazel eyes. They glowered disapprovingly at us and while we did not understand a word of their "clucking", we knew they mocked us, that they disliked us, and made fun of Dad's half-breed kids. When we became old enough to say "no" to Dad's invitations to go see Uncle Jimmy, eventually even Dad stopped going. We never contacted that side of his family again.

Grandpa Harry died in 1963 in a poor tenement in San Francisco's Chinatown. He died a poor and nearly penniless man who was bitter to the end, never having achieved the respect he always thought was his due. It was the last time I remember seeing the chicken women clucking as they told us where to stand during his funeral. I recall there was no peace on Harry's cardboard-colored face as he lay in his coffin. He looked mean even in death. He was buried at the large Chinese cemetery in Colma, California. For Harry and his five sons, there was no returning to China, no land of inheritance, and no legacy to pass on.

Our mother, understandably, never saw Harry again since the day she chased him around the house wielding a meat cleaver. Our father would tell her what the Yee Family was up to on occasion, even though Mom never asked.

In 1954, the Red Guard swept through the country sides of China, even to the very remote villages. Composed of mostly beautiful young people, some merely children, they marched into cities, towns and eventually small rural villages, spreading the good word and works of a Socialist Chinese People's Republic where all would work together, equal in their powers and free to work for the good of one another. All people were equal now, freedom and liberation had arrived at last, they cried and sang. Their marches inevitably found their way into the small countryside Yee Village, where an old, frail and wizen crone still spent her days and nights controlling the lives of those who served her in feudal allegiance.

As in past cities, towns and villages, the Red Guard swiftly moved to demonstrate the political changes that would set these people free from all those who believed they were rightful landlords. This land would now belong to the People of China, and everything the land produced would be shared equally among its people. To demonstrate this, the Villagers were called to gather around a hillside, where all could witness the changing of the guard. Over her vocal objections, two youth took the old crone from her house and half-carried and half-walked her up the hillside, and when they reached the top, they began to make beautiful, bright and energetic speeches. As red banners waved in the mid-morning breeze, and as generations of her subjects watched, the youth in the khaki shirts and red bandanas and simple caps with red stars on them, stripped the old woman of her silk embroidered clothes down to her undergarments, and forced my father's old Ni-Ni to kneel in broken glass. This proved to all that she was no longer in charge nor ruled over anyone. She would be sent to a "rehabilitation camp" to learn the new philosophies of a new China. There, she would die a broken woman, with no available family to mourn her passing, to ceremoniously bury her, nor inherit anything from her world. The pile of life's regrets was buried with her bones.

    The other side of our Family was little different. My Mother's mother lived in Sierra Madre and retired from Lockheed-Martin in Pasadena. Her husband (our Irish/Welsh grandfather) died of cancer in 1960. He was a kind and gentle man who, in his lifetime, never stood up to his wife. And as a widow, she never remarried. She remained a stern and opinionated woman who still dominated the lives of her other two children, even as adults. My Irish Grandmother's relationship with my mother was wholly different. There was a truce, but no peace. There was reluctant acceptance, and cool indifference. My

Mother spent the whole of her life trying to get back into the good graces of her mother, and failed.

Once, on a visit to her 'mother's home in Southern California, Mom took her oldest first-born daughter, now married. My sister was excited to show off her new baby boy. My oldest sister married a full-blooded American-born Chinese, and her baby son was now three-quarters Asian. He had beautiful thick black hair, cut in a "rice-bowl" haircut, big dark eyes and a beautiful dimpled smile. As my sister walked her baby son out to the front of the house with her grandmother showing off her roses and plants, a neighbor happened to approach. The neighbor asked my Irish Grandmother if she had company. Grandma was caught off guard quickly introduced my sister, not as her rightful granddaughter, but as a "friend of the Family." To the end of her life, my Irish Grandmother could not reconcile nor admit the mix of Asian blood in her Family blood lines. It still brought her shame.

We rarely had contact with any of our Irish relatives during our growing up years. We perhaps met our cousins once or twice. As adults, we acknowledged each other with some mutual amusement but never bonded. We remained strangers really. Our childhood, our very lives were lived out on a virtual island, isolating us from possible painful judgments from both sides.

In 1990, at the age of seventy, my father announced to his Family that he was ready to become an American citizen. Some years earlier, during the Kennedy Administration in the early 1960's, two federal agents of the Bureau of Immigration and Naturalization knocked on our door. All of us kids were asked to leave the house or go to our rooms. The agents questioned my dad about his immigration into the United States, and then proceeded to reveal that a fire had destroyed pertinent INS documentation for that time period, and it was feared no documents now existed to corroborate his story. In the interim, the United States Government was willing to admit fault in this matter and issued a permanent green card status to Dad until he should decide to become a U.S. citizen. With this card, he was able to earn Social Security, work using his former Social Security Number, and do everything except vote. It took him thirty more years to decide he wanted to vote. His children schooled him, making flash cards for his memorization, making him repeat key points of American history. We took him to fill out the paperwork, and on the day of his swearing in ceremony, he was the only one, among a small group of émigrés, who stood up and yelled "Yippee!" as he waved his small hand-held American Flag.

In 1994, Mom and Dad passed away within three months of each other. That year was filled with endless pain mixed with appropriate grieving, gratitude and expected sadness. At our mother's funeral, Lincoln Memorial had opened the double crypt and at the gravesite, was prepared to insert her coffin in front of Daddy's coffin, when the Funeral Director paused and lifted his gaze up to the tree-lined hill above us. There, in the beautiful morning's light, stood a female deer and a large male buck, his antlers majestic on his head. "Will you look at that! In all my years here I've never seen that before," the funeral director said. "There's some symbolism if ever I saw it," he added. "What do you mean?" I asked. We were all standing there staring up the hill watching the perfect pair look down at us. "I would say your parents have gone on before you, as it should be," he said, turning back to help insert mother's coffin.

Despite the heavy wool cloth of my overcoat, the cold of the granite bench seeped into my backside as I sat down in front of their crypt. It was the July 4th weekend, and yet summer was not to be found here in Portland, Oregon. The skies were grey and heavy-laden with moisture in the clouds. It was a typical day for the Great Northwest. There was a wind that rounded the corners of the twenty-foot wall of crypts, and it found me where I sat staring at the brass names of my parents. **David L. Fong and Laura M. Fong**, followed by their birth and death dates.

I am their daughter, Kathryn, the third child, the last of the girl children before the three boys came into the world. Mother had eight pregnancies, and six live births: first, three girls, and then three boys. I teased her that it was "planned parenthood" by design. It was my first introduction to true irony when I learned she never wanted children.

I remember the cold. I jammed my hands deep inside my pockets and bent closer to my lower half in a huddle against the effects of wind and damp. It had been not quite four weeks since my siblings and I buried our mother here. She and Daddy were now interred in this wall crypt in a cozy symbiosis that would allow their bodies to return to dust in a simple dry, bug-free and weather-proofed environment for the dead. I (we were) still struggling with Mother's death so very soon after burying our father less than four months earlier. Daddy died in February, and Mother died in May. It didn't just rock us from our feet, it laid us out low and even with the ground.

Mother had earlier picked out a double wall crypt designed to hold two caskets as we prepared for Father's inevitable death. Because of his advanced cancer, we knew it was coming soon, so we took Mom up to the cemetery to make all the arrangements ahead of time. We felt it would ease the grieving process if we didn't have to think about the details after his death. All the arrangements were made in advance. Daddy would be buried first and inserted into the double crypt feet first, so that his head was at the middle of the crypt. Both their names would be in brass outside the wall, waiting only for Mother's death date to be added at the appropriate time. When Mom passed away, the Funeral Director said the crypt would be re-opened, and her casket would be inserted head first, so that both their heads would be somewhat together for all eternity. The thought pleased Mom as she pictured her and Dad lying head-to-head as though gazing up at the stars together, or holding a conversation lying on a picnic blanket, so she signed all the papers making it so. No one knew that less than three months later, she would join him in that eternal position, and with the brass dates completed, they would be entombed, head-to-head, as their mortal remains turned to dust. No one ever knows these things.

I sat there numbing up to the cold and staring at their brass names and dates: two deaths three months apart. Friends and Family said it happens a lot like that. Everyone's response was the same no matter who I spoke with. Once I had told someone both my parents died three months apart, their response would be like this: *"That happens when two people have such a deep and abiding love. They can't live without each other,"* they'd say. *"It's something to do with losing their will to live. The other mate just can't go on without the other." "Death cannot end such a great love as theirs."*

It was rubbish, nonsense really. I refused to believe it. Those people didn't live with them. They didn't see how these two carried on day after day as husband and wife. I did. I lived with them as a child, and for the last ten years of their lives, they lived with me as an adult while I took care of them!

My brothers and sisters grew up with them, as I did. We knew them as their children, and we cared for them as adults. We all witnessed their almost daily squabbles, their constant bickering and their mutual disrespect. True love transcends even the bonds of death? In this case, it just was *not* true. Whatever kept them together for forty-eight years, I was entirely convinced it was not love.

So, there I was, trying to find shelter in a windy crypt corridor, staring at Mom and Dad's final resting place, trying to imagine them, now and forever, locked in a head-to-head confrontation that would most certainly wake the dead that surrounded them. I imagined their eternal bickering driving the mortal remains of those closest to their crypt to rise up and complain to Management that their eternal rest had been violated by my recently departed Mother and Father. My mind went to an even funnier scene of marble crypt covers bursting forward, and the rise and echo of moaning and groaning corpses breaking free of their eternal confines, all rushing for the nearest exit just to escape the bitter banter of my dearly departed. I smiled to think that Mother's design for a double crypt was a bitter plot to keep their battles going for the rest of eternity.

It's funny what grief does to some people. I wanted to very much believe that love did exist for Mom and Dad. But I argued against it furiously, like a prosecuting attorney before a high court.

"Your Honor, if I may, I am prepared to unequivocally prove without a shadow of doubt, that Laura could not possibly love David. She never did, and your Honor, never will! By the time I am finished presenting evidence, there will be no jury in the land who will doubt or disbelieve that love does not exist in their relationship. How could it, your Honor? Under the circumstances, knowing the truth of their relationship, their forty-eight years together, how can one accuse them of a loving

marriage?"

After all, I knew them better than anyone else, didn't I? I agreed to let them move in with me after they retired ten years earlier. I agreed to care for them, pay their bills, give them shelter and things to do in their senior years. While those ten years were filled with happy memories, good times and bad, the level of combativeness was endless and remarkable. My two sisters and I laughed over how often we had to separate them, like two willful, offending children. We would order them to separate rooms. We had to pull the car over and threaten to turn around and take them home if the fighting did not stop. We would praise and reward them when they managed a kindness, or stifled a rude comment. It was like raising two bratty, contentious kids.

But here I was, in front of their grave marker, not hearing a whisper of complaint or disparaging remark, and I was remembering. I remembered the bright spring day we took them both to see the breathless beauty of a nearby rhododendron garden in May. Many plants were over fifty and hundred years old, and in full regaling bloom. We picnicked there, and as my sisters and I played games with their grandchildren, we spied Mom and Dad walking hand-in-hand, like lovers do, to sit near the lake and watch the ducks. Yes, there it was. Wasn't that a loving tender moment of the heart? Didn't we just glimpse love?

What about the time, shortly after Dad was diagnosed with terminal cancer, I came home from work and found them on the backyard deck, saying goodbye to the setting sun, yet another day gone. They were holding each other's hand across the table and sitting in serene silence. There it was again. Wasn't that love I just saw? I had glimpses, didn't I?

But the old argument would rise inside of me with that shadow of doubt witness for the prosecution. *"These few loving demonstrations, your Honor, over a lifetime of bitter and acrimonious exchange were not a loving marriage made. This can't be love."*

My butt was numb now, and the cold was beginning to meld with my core temperature to the point that I no longer seemed to feel its affects. I continued to stare at their crypt. I had cried a boat load of tears for these two people. I mourned them so deeply that I felt my own heart left me for dead. I was deprived of sleep, deprived of peace, deprived of both my parents. They were dead, and not unlike the living, I needed answers. The eighteen months it took for our father to die was a living hell. It was the nightmare of the dying, and I was a helpless witness. To have Mom die so soon after Dad, was as though my skin had been stripped from my body by the inch. How could such pain exist? Why did I care so much, after years and years of hearing them argue and fight? Why did I love these two when so very little love seemed to exist between them? Who were these two that they could exact so much from my heart, my mind and my spirit? My life was deathly quiet now; peace could enter my life at last. Why did I not open that door and let it in? I realized that in order to allow peace in my life, I needed to find and defend the love my parents had for each other. I needed to find that love, understand that love and celebrate their lives because of that love. If their own child could not defend them in life, I could do so in their deaths, knowing that with all my heart, David did indeed, love Laura. Or so I needed to believe.

I had to find out why. But the "why" was perhaps the most difficult to discover. My Father was of Chinese descent, and my blond, blue-eyed Mother was of Irish and English heritage. It wasn't enough to explain why these two met and fell in love sufficiently to defy their families and marry at the height of

World War II. There appeared to be very little sanity in their decision to marry. How would I discover the depths of their love from this?

They married without the approval of their families. No surprise there. They were forced to marry in another state because California (for all its liberalness today) then had laws preventing interracial marriage. They ran off on the 24th day of March, 1945 to Gallup, New Mexico for a civil ceremony at city hall. Despite the disapproval of their parents, defying the advice of their friends, and in the face of a Society that would spurn and punish them for their decision, these two married each other. To marry meant they could not live without the other in their lives. The realities that awaited them when they returned to Southern California could not prevent or diminish the love that demanded this apparent and, in many respects, unlawful and forbidden union.

They knew, from personal experience, what prejudice was and what it felt like. Bigotry was apparent in the smiles of people with dead eyes, the double, sideways glances, the fingers not too shy to point in their direction, and the unintentional/intentional judgments that came speedily, without censure and without aforethought. Father was a gregarious man always in search of a good story and a laugh, but in his desire to win you over, he waited, he hesitated long enough to discern if you could be a friend or just another bigoted enemy prepared to dismiss him. He and Mother knew what it was like to be the objects of ridicule, hate, and conflict.

I had once asked our Caucasian uncle, who was the last surviving member of our mother's family, why his older sister married our father. He was witness to the time and place. He quickly told me that he 'was not actually at home, he was a soldier somewhere in the Pacific theater of World War II at the time they married. I was certain his family, even perhaps friends from home, must have written him about this. He grew silent, judging whether to be honest with me about how his family felt about my mother's choice of husbands. I decided to let him off the hook, and said I could only imagine what his mother and father must have felt about this marriage, but what I really wanted him to tell me is what was my mother thinking, what was her rationale? Did she offer any reasonable, sound justification for choosing my father as her intended? Uncle's reply was that he had never thought about it nor did he question his sister about it. He 'did not recall any deep discussions, any attempt at interventions. It was her choice, and Laura Mae was like that, defiant and stubborn, he said. I continued to press, "But this was at the height of the war. White women didn't choose Asian men. Asians, whether Chinese or Japanese, were not looked kindly on during this time in history. What logical explanation did they have for their families to marry? She dated lots of Caucasian soldiers and sailors. Why not one of them?"

Uncle grew silent again, weighing his thoughts, and struggling for words. "She always told me all they wanted was to get into her pants, and she didn't want to. She told me David was not like that. He treated her like a lady. She liked that about him. And if she was going to marry, it was going to be her choice, and nothing could stop her."

So, there was Uncle's perspective: Mom was trying to remain chaste, and Daddy was a gallant gentleman with her. It was not a satisfying answer. I tried to imagine how a young girl of 20 could initiate a relationship with a twenty-two-year-old Chinese man during a world war against Japan and Germany. America held captive every Japanese American citizen in the country. Daddy had to confine himself to the borders of Los Angeles' Old Chinatown, and he had to wear an "I AM CHINESE" yellow button on his jacket to prevent being hassled on the streets of LA by would-be patriotic zealots. Chinatown had a curfew for all Chinese at nine p.m. each night, and still, my father and his cousins were often harassed or beaten by vigilante Americans.

I recalled a time when I was quite young, perhaps eight years old, I asked my mother why she married Daddy. I was becoming aware of what it felt to be a child of two cultures. We were what the Chinese called "A-B-C's," or American Born Chinese. But not really. We were also known as half-breeds. *Multicultural* was not a by-word for my generation. We were from a mixed-marriage, and that made us "half-breeds" in those days. Mother married outside the boundaries of Society, and Daddy married up. We all felt the sting of hatred, bigotry and dismissive attitudes. We had no outside Family who acknowledged us from either the Chinese or White side. We had few family friends and fewer neighbors who would accept us. I was now aware of how strangers responded to us on streets and in stores. But maybe my own Mother didn't understand this racial prejudice. If she did, why would she have married my father? So, I asked her, "Mom, why did you marry Daddy?" I asked. "What?" she said, as though she didn't understand the question. "Why did you and Dad marry each other?" Her facial expression changed, her eyes moving closer together in a *cross-with-me* squint. "Why do you want to know that for?" she challenged. "As a couple, you're a bit unusual," I ventured back to her, trying to avoid her 'stink-eye'. Like most moms she wasn't happy at taking cheek from her child, and she dismissed me with a wave of her hand and a turn of her eyes away from me. "That's a stupid question," she countered.

"But why?" I pressed. A pause expressed itself in the air between us. Finally, she said, "I don't know; because I loved him." she said with irritated voice. I knew little more than when I started.

I think I asked my father the same question and he acted in the same annoyed way she did. I was apparently stupid for asking such a stupid question.

But I wasn't stupid enough to understand, even from an early age, ours was not the typical Donna Reed family. I had three brothers and two older sisters and I saw, we all saw, how people looked at us. We knew we were not an average American Family in the Fifties and Sixties growing up. Our school mates found it difficult to size us up. Were we Spanish? Were we Korean, Japanese, Hawaiian? Someone said we looked French? The dark hair, the olive complexion, the white complexion and the brown and hazel green eyes did nothing to assert our apparent heritage and where we fit in. They tried to measure us by our last name of "Fong" which devolved into "Fing-Fong", "Fong-Chong" and a host of bad derivations. We stood out, and kids know when they are made to feel different. To this day as an adult, I still have wonderful life-long friends who call me simply 'Fong'.

I remembered how my mom would be forced to defend and explain her last name to people. *"Fong?" "That sounds Asian." "What country is that name from?" "Oh! It's Chinese." "Then your husband is from China?" "How interesting."* Generally, conversations thinned after this revelation and drifted or died away. I watched Mother squirm during these interactions, and her body would become rigid and defensive. Her little white nose would incline upwards a few degrees. It was a learned behavior based on countless of thoughtless and hurtful prejudices levied at her. She never seemed prepared enough for the back-handed and disguised bigotry of others she met. Her normal defense always appeared to me to be 'duck and run'.

In general, my sisters and I were treated kindlier by schoolmates and adults. For some reason, we represented sweet little girls, and judgments and criticisms and outright bigotry became whispers not intended for our ears. But our three younger brothers felt it every day of their young lives. While they made friends, others would tease them, pick fights with them and push them around, and some adults outwardly chose to taunt them for their mixed heritage. The world of males was a bit rougher, and men were never discreet in their conversations with other males.

I did not confront, nor understand, the burden of prejudice from the 1940's, but I did understand and had to confront the 50's and 60's and decades beyond that. The one revelation for me was that White people could never imitate nor come close to the levels of prejudice expressed by the Chinese. Chinese had thousands of more year's practice in their intolerance for White Westerners. You have no idea.

White Western society grew up reflecting the philosophies and beliefs of their family, their roots and the people and regions they come from. What was taught is that people who are different from you, not the same as you, are worthy to be ignored, kicked around, abused and considered beneath you. To that nth degree, white people felt empowered by these beliefs to either ignore the problem of non-acceptable society by ignoring them with distain, or hurling abuse in the form of poor word choices or physical violence or both.

Now, if you happened to have been born Chinese, with a long, long, long history of Chinese ancestry and familial cultural influence, you learn to hate what is beneath you. You don't ignore it, you actively resort to eradicating it from your presence. You don't just tolerate it, you either use it to your advantage (such as paying off the local police to look the other way when laws are broken.) You smile politely to shield your hatred. You feign respect all the while you seethe with hate inside you. You know in your heart that you are so far above these retched white folk that it is beneath you to even breath their air.

    I once worked with a young intern at my office when I was still in my twenties in the early 1970's. She was only 19, a student from Stanford University, working for us for the summer months. She was a full-blooded ABC, born to a rich family whose father was a renowned surgeon admired by many of his colleagues. I learned from her that she had a "secret" love going on with a White American student her age. She was nervous and upset when he pressured her to meet her parents at a large party being held to honor her father, the doctor. "I can't introduce him," she declared to me. "My Father would kill me if he found out we were dating," she said. "Introduce him as a 'friend' then," I offered. "You don't understand, my father hates all white people!" her voice rising for emphasis. "The people invited to this party are co-workers he tolerates for the sake of his career, but he silently hates them. He wouldn't just punish me, if he knew I loved Thomas, he would have me killed before allowing me to date or, God-forbid, marry him." I was dumbfounded, and yet here in the 1970's she confirmed what I long suspected about the depths of hatred many Chinese had for White people. Many White people are racist thinkers, but Chinese are racist doers. The story of why my mother chased Harry around the house with a meat cleaver (which did happen) serves as a wicked reminder of Chinese evil intent. Equally, the story of the restaurant cooks peeing into the Chinese dishes they were preparing for the police officers, while a fictional illustration of the kind of contempt they had for American law enforcement, it is not far from the truth when I say how much they hated White Authority.

Then, if I knew prejudice, and she knew prejudice, why, WHY did she marry Daddy? Was all the love in the world enough to make that kind of challenge worthwhile back in 1945? Was love worth all this pain and ridicule and unending bigotry by others?

Each of the remaining six siblings dealt with their emotions individually and alone. We did not seem to want to come together to collectively heal. We licked our wounds by ourselves, and it cost us the ties that once bound us and labeled us as a Family. Most of us sought temporary counseling and turned to limited amounts of Diazepam to help us through our mourning. This eventually turned to other activities to fill our void. Life went on.

I played golf nearly every day. My brothers quickly resumed their lives and routines, not seeming to be much phased by our loss. But our oldest sister worked on a revelatory story that shocked us all. In a poorly written, and hastily put together manuscript in which she placed a collage of photos of Mom and Dad, and neatly bound it all in a plastic and paper folio, she told us, in story-form, a huge secret the rest of her brothers and sisters knew nothing about. Dad had married a Chinese woman while on his last visit to China and fathered another child. He was a boy. We had another brother, even if by another woman. My sister accused our father of bigamy and said in her story that Mom and Dad, while they were living with me, received a letter one day, addressed to our father from a man living in San Francisco.

Dad was devastated to read in that letter that his "other" son and his "other" wife had emigrated to the United States and were settling in with the help of "cousins." The man, my father's Chinese son, appealed to my father to do the right thing and help them by sending money so they could live comfortably in San

Francisco. The son further appealed for compassion and financial support by pointing out in his letter than his mother, Dad's Chinese wife, was not well and needed medical attention. After all these years, the son begged for the support of a father he did not know nor had ever met. The letter must have ended with a question of "will you help us?"

I was the daughter who took care of my parents after they retired. We all lived in a house that the three of us shared. I paid the bills. I knew how little money they received from Social Security as their retirement. Yet, in all this, I did not know about this letter.

Mom and Dad apparently burned the letter. They measured the words in the letter against their fears, and their fear won out. They could not help anyone. If they did, Dad might be arrested for bigamy. If he was arrested, his pension and retirement income might be taken away. Worse, they might have to repay the government for falsifying documents. Even worse, the son and the other wife might come up to Oregon and presume to live happily with us. So, they burned the letter. They told my oldest sister but did not tell anyone else, not even me, their caregiver.

My two sisters waited impatiently, as I read this stunning revelation a month after Mother's funeral. My sisters both ate an entire bowl of chocolate that sat between them as I sat across the room and read this invective accusation.

"Well," they asked me, anxious for my reaction as I set the manuscript down, "what do you think?"

I was closed. "What do you want me to think?" I asked.

"Dad was a bigamist! We have a half-brother living somewhere in this country! Aren't you devastated?"

"By what?" I countered.

"Dad was a liar and a cheat. What part of 'bigamist' don't

you understand?" My sisters were disappointed by the flatness of my reaction.

"If you stop to think about why he did this, it makes this story more comprehensible," I offered. I didn't want to give this diatribe of hers any foundation.

Our Father was forced by a cruel and strong-willed woman whom he called "Ni-Ni." She was willful, ruthless and selfish. She purchased Dad as a baby to provide her own comforts and to thwart her husband and five sons. When our father had returned to China, for the last time, she took the opportunity to seize him, to hold him until he complied with her wishes. Her demands were to force him into a Chinese marriage in order to eradicate the unacceptable marriage he had made in another part of the world. And to a White Demon, no less! This was the conspiracy brewed up by Harry and his Chinese wife. Her dominant will was more than my father could stand up against. If he was to have any chance of escaping her, he had to feign obedience. Though, in his own mind, the marriage to a Chinese woman he did not know was a sham, he calculated that if he could appease his Ni-Ni, he would eventually be able to make his way to the coast of China and find a ship bound for San Francisco. By Chinese standards, China allowed polygamy among those who could afford the bride price. My father's compliance was to save his real marriage by deception, and possibly even to save his own life in the end.

My sisters were shocked. In my refusal to see Dad as a law-breaker, a miscreant and a bad father and husband, they turned away from me to avoid more conflict. We were torn in our pledges to his memory.

I understand why he might have done this, and later, I understood the fear both might have had about exposing this awful secret to all their children. They could not face the bitterness and possible feelings of betrayal, nor risk such an exposure to those who might prosecute them under our country's laws.

One thing I did agree with my two sisters on was what it did to our mother. I never knew the feisty, stubborn fighter who rebelled against an entire world when it did not support her marriage to an Asian. I was born as a result of my Father escaping from China and returning home to his White wife. The woman I grew up knowing was far different from the woman who chose to marry our father.

The news of what he did while in China changed my mother's life. It did more than that. It sucked away her air and ate away at the life she thought she had, and though she stayed married to this man for forty-eight years, and had five more pregnancies, Mother's life-force ebbed and waned with each passing year. The hurt and pain and guilt were too much to bear, and her pride and spirit were broken.

She increasingly gave up. In my lifetime, I never knew her to dress up or care for her appearance except on rare occasions. She lost her beautiful smile and large white teeth. She went from her bed, to her chair, to her sofa and back to bed on most days. My brothers and sisters, in our clumsy and inadequate way, took care of the housekeeping and general cooking. She never attended any of us in our school activities, nor our school pageants or programs, or when any of us were found worthy of awards and school accolades. She never saw any of her sons play school football, basketball or field and track sports.

She was tender. She was weak. She was often sick. In the quietness of her own mind, she played it over and over and over, and found that life was indeed, miserable. The depression led to her physical weaknesses, and those led to her inevitable demise.

Had she forgiven Dad? I think so. I saw glimpses of their love, and it was enough for me to know that these two loved each other. They were known to hold hands in their last years together. They often had quiet conversations meant only for them. Their love may have been crushed and mangled and misshapen by those who conspired against them, but they loved each other. They were, in their way, affectionate on occasion. Whether it might have been better for them to divorce and to live separate lives was not something we could dictate. It was theirs to decide, and they chose each other, no matter what of the past seeped into the future, they chose each other. To die so close together, less than three months apart, was, perhaps, a real demonstration of that love we did not understand.

Shortly after Mom's funeral, while in my grieving state, I accepted a work assignment to travel to New York to conduct some business. I was staying in an old hotel in the lower east side of Manhattan near Wall Street. The building was once apartments and now, as a hotel, they offered old rooms complete with kitchenettes, small refrigerators, old counter tops and a windowed sink that looked out on to tall business buildings surrounding this short ten story tenement hotel.

Still reeling from my devastating loss, I fell into a fitful sleep from my bed that faced that old kitchen. My last view as I closed my weary eyes was of the beautifully-lit office buildings outside that kitchen window in downtown Manhattan. As my eyelids succumbed to their heaviness, the lights outside became jewels. As I fell asleep, I dreamed.

In that dream, I was awakened by dishes rattling and water running. I sat up, eyes bleary and tired and saw my father under a single and dim overhead light, washing dishes and softly whistling a happy tune.

"Daddy!" I came out of bed. "What are you doing here?"

He did not answer me, but continued to wash and rinse dishes in that little sink. I watched incredulously, smiling at his sweet countenance. I noted he was smiling too, seemingly enjoying the sundry task in his hands. I knew he did not belong here and as I contemplated the ethereal meaning of this visitation, I heard footsteps behind me.

I turned toward the sound of those heavy footfalls and found them unmistakably familiar to me. It was Mom! As soon as my mind confirmed for me that Mother was coming toward us, the walls of my small Manhattan apartment drew back and like a game show contestant, she entered this strange stage from the wings.

"Mom!" I cried. My whole soul leapt to impossible heights. Mother ignored my exclamation and walked swiftly and purposefully passed me. Apparently, I was only a witness to this Family reunion, and not a participant.

Dad turned to Mom just as she reached him, and the two embraced, and kissed. I must tell you, dear reader, that I've seen my parents kiss before, many times. But this was a kiss that I knew was meant to heal my grieving soul. They kissed like I never seen them kiss before in this life. They kissed as though they would never be parted again. They kissed as though no other love could have existed but this. They kissed, and all the pain, all the grief, all the wrongs, the hurts and betrayals left the building. They kissed because love existed. They kissed, and I knew they loved.

They kissed.

Was it a dream, or was it a gift? I withdrew from their company as though I did not belong in that room where they were, even though it was my room. My mind ended this scenario by swiftly moving me into another dream which ultimately did not matter.

Upon waking, I marveled at my vision dream. What was the meaning of such a dream? I could only surmise its meaning by the way it made me feel. My heart was lighter, my sadness lifted. I could believe, for once in my life that real love, meaningful love, could exist and, indeed, did exist for my mother and my father. I could embrace the thought that once upon a time, two people defied a world and came together despite all odds. What they did, what they survived, what obstacles blocked their path were all overcome by the weight and the power and the strength of their love for each other. The kiss in that dream was my confirmation. It was a brief and beautiful glimpse of the truth of their lives together. It was validation.

Two people, different in every way, came together, despite the objection of an entire world, and chose to live a life together. They chose to raise up their Family, and cling to one another until death did them part. I more than witnessed their lives, I now understood it. I now could understand their journey. It all made sense to me now. Love can conquer. It can overcome. It can set a soul on fire sufficient to shut out the bitter and bigoted rantings of friends and family, and especially strangers. And it can burn, this fire, for a *very, very* long time.

In the end, after loved ones pass away, our memories are altered in kind ways which allow forgiveness and understanding to enter our hearts. All the bad times, the unhappy memories, the awful things that came between you, and the parents who raised you, are somehow burned away, leaving only love and understanding. Nothing else matters. Just the love, and a final acceptance that despite their flaws, faults and poor decisions, they were human beings doing the best they could.

Forgiveness is all that is left when everything else is gone.

My parents were not perfect. Most are not. In their weaknesses, I claimed many obstacles of my own to overcome, and my life was significantly shaped by what I endured as their child. My parents were not good parents. Many are not. But in our home, we gathered together, supported each other, stood by each other, and made our way together the best we knew how. We were an island Family, not belonging to anything or anyone who would not tolerate us.

Many people refused to show us any kindness or tolerance. Many wonderful people did. We had friends. We had good neighbors. We had those whose lives were bright enough to not judge us and who accepted us for who we were. I dedicate this book to all of them. I will be a witness for them before the Courts on High. I thank them all for the example of what it means to live in a free and loving Society, where colors blend into happy mediums that make up the shades of human life. Prejudice was once a collective association. A long time ago, societal dictates were normal. You simply had to conduct yourself in such a manner to be found "acceptable" or "normal." But now, in the 21st century, prejudice has become a singular and most individual blight. Where life was once intolerant, stiff-necked and prohibitive, it now moves more freely within itself. It now is expressed without words and levied by a glance of dismissal. Don't misunderstand. Prejudice and bigotry still exist. Why else, in this age of beauty and progressiveness, does Hollywood still hire White actors to play Asian roles in the industry? While it still exists, we carry our condemnation of other people not like us, silently and without exposure. Prejudice has become an awkward and silent thing that hangs between people like a sheet of white wall that separates two individuals or groups of people. We simply ignore others that don't appeal to our sense of right. Instead of signs that declare "Colored sit here" our prejudice is now unspoken, gone underground, hiding behind a big, unapologetic smile. But the world has changed; is changing! It won't always be like this.

We can change; we need to change. Instead of bleaching out color, we need to embrace it, invite it and stand side-by-side with color and races from all around this world until we no longer see any color. No difference. Just people.

Where interracial marriages were once banned, today doors are open to "multicultural" weddings. Multi-ethnic socialism struggles to seed itself everywhere. The older generations strain to smile and accept the relationships their youth bring home. We learn from our mistakes. We grow from there. We reach out and beyond the once tiny microcosm of our existence. It is a prerequisite life lesson and a glimpse into Heaven.

Generations of mankind have filled this earth, and it may even be possible for each of us to trace our ancestry back to Adam and Eve. It makes the billions of people who have gone before real, their lives tangible. We are linked together in order and lineage. It is a rich tapestry of heritage and inheritance. But I also see that my parents' lives were all too brief, and the candle of their combined lives extinguished much too early. I also see the irony of our deaths in their lives. You see, my brothers had no sons. Our family name will not survive, and it will burn itself out with the dying of the last sibling. The other younger generations of our family's lineage will inherit fewer and fewer aspects of our blended bloodlines. Where I, and my sisters and brothers claim half of our father's blood and half of our 'mother's blood, one day, David and Laura's line will diminish to mere molecules. Those who inherit one-quarter, then one-eighth and then one-sixteenth of our blood will never know what it means to be a half-breed. Hopefully, they will never witness the struggle, the persecution, the trials and triumphs of loving a forbidden love. For the world we know, and the world they will come to know, will be different. The world is more embracing. The world is more tolerant. There will come a day when people, despite their color and appearance, will be homogenous, blended and looked upon by others as the same members of humanity and social status, equal to themselves. For this, we must thank the pioneers, like David and Laura (and many others like them) who broke down walls, overcame barriers and withstood the attacks and injustices heaped upon them. They taught us how to stand up and withstand. We are now free to reach out, free to choose, free to love.

This, above all, is our lasting inheritance, and their legacy. We are all free to love whoever claims our hearts.

Thanks Mom and Dad, for pioneering that brave new world; no longer forbidden.

The End

Here he is about seventeen years of age.

We, of course, have no photographs of Daddy before his teen years. Cameras did not exist in the China village of his youth, and no one thought of taking his photograph when he was a boy under Harry's rule.

My Father had an ego, even for the third-class citizen that he was in the 1930's. He loved American clothing, and with his limited income as a houseboy working at the Home of Ramona/Caldera Rancho in Valencia, California, he did the best he could.

A smoker since his youth, Father would smoke for fifty years, and finally, one day after I made a fuss over a cigarette burn in our linen tablecloth, he quit smoking. I marveled at how both mom and he quit their two packs a day smoking cold turkey, without cheating and without looking back. It gave me a glimpse of their inner strengths and resolve, even during a time I believed them to be very weak people. That was a beautiful time during their non-smoking last few years together.

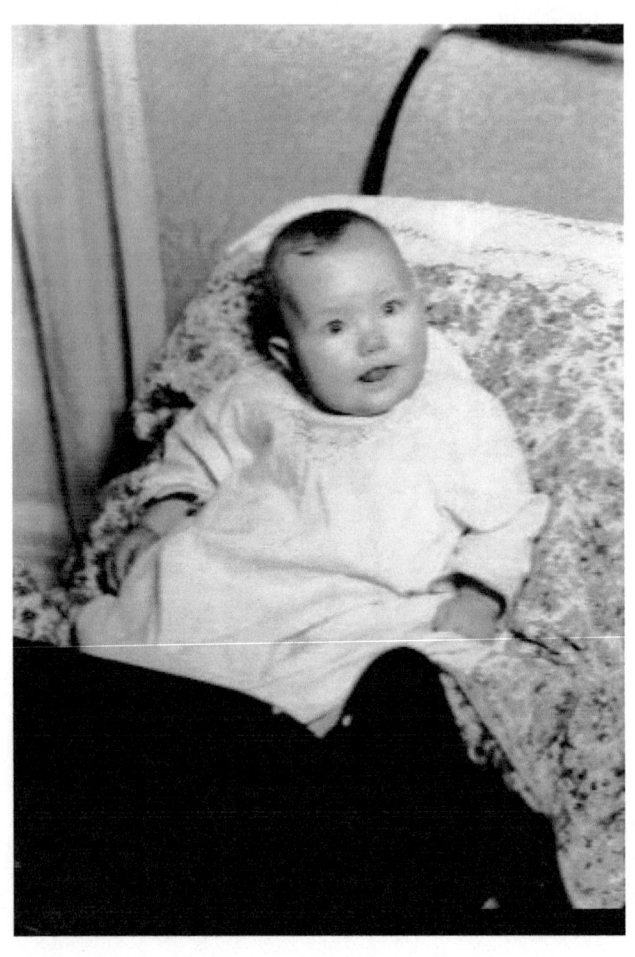

Mom four to six months old.

This one always reminded me of a children's fairy tale of a girl forced to sweep by her wicked step-mother. Look at her little boots!

Was there ever a hint of that fiery Irish temper? Could we see a glimpse of that rebellious nature, and her "don't tell me what to do with my life!" attitude?

Mother, age seventeen, perhaps a bit older, graduating from High School.

The young woman emerges…

Mom (on the right) was a blond beauty. Here she is with her best friend Margi. The 1940's gave her power in independence and purpose which galvanized most of Americans during World War II. To a great degree the war empowered all women in America. Mother worked in a factory assembling crystal radio sets for the United States Army.

Mother (center) enjoyed clubbing with her young friends, and as you can see, the boys in uniform had a difficult time keeping their eyes (and hands) off her. You can almost hear the Big Band era music performing in the background.

They had to go to New Mexico to be legally married. California (circa 1945) did not permit interracial marriage.

The only photograph we have of their honeymoon, March 1945. An Asian friend, albeit a pilot and Colonel, William Huang of the U.S. Army, flew Mom and Dad to New Mexico, and acted as a witness to their civil ceremony.

New Parents, Mom and Dad take turns holding their first-born daughter 1946.

Daddy with his three girls in Salinas, California, where we were born. I am holding his hand, and my two sisters are sitting at the base of the flagpole.

Now getting older, with six children to support, Dad was no longer a fashion-plate.

Mother often wore her grief on her face. Suffering from depression, she grew heavy with disillusionment and the weariness of life, and for a woman who never wanted kids, six of them took a lot of wind out of her sails.

Life is nearing its end when we snapped this photo; this is Mom at Daddy's funeral. She would follow him to her own grave less than four months later.